Axolotl Facts for Kids
The Ultimate Guide for Children & Parents

Axpone Press

Published by Axpone Press

Copyright © 2025 by Axpone Press

All rights reserved.

No part of this book may be reproduced in any form or by any electronic or mechanical means, including information storage and retrieval systems, without written permission from the author, except for the use of brief quotations in a book review.

IngramSpark ISBN: 978-1-915363-66-4

Cover design courtesy of a contest on 99designs.com. For more information, please contact the publisher.

The following stock images are used with licenses purchased from Adobe Stock: ASSET ID: *#473131207 & #281813132*

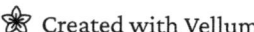

Contents

Introduction	v
1. What Makes Axolotls So Cool?	1
Draw the Life Cycle of an Axolotl!	23
2. Axolotl Behavior and Communication	24
3. What do Axolotls Eat?	32
4. Caring for Your Pet Axolotl	38
5. Keeping Axolotls Healthy	50
6. Axolotls in Legends and Stories	61
7. Axolotls in the Wild Today	71
8. Are You Ready to Own an Axolotl?	80
9. Easy Axolotl Quiz	86
10. The Hard Axolotl Quiz!	90
11. The Fun Axolotl Quiz...	94
12. Answers: Easy Axolotl Quiz	99
13. Answers: The Hard Axolotl Quiz	105
14. Answers: The Fun Axolotl Quiz	110
Afterword	117

Introduction

'*Axolotl Facts for Kids*' will explain why these special, Mexican salamanders are so cool, how they live in the wild, and how to keep them as pets. It's the best Axolotl book in existence!

In recent years, axolotls have become an internet sensation. Everyone who surfs the internet or uses social media is familiar with their sweet, smiling faces with their fancy, frilly gills and tiny hands. But there is much, much more to axolotls than Minecraft or TikTok posts, as we will reveal.

This complete guide is not just for owners or people thinking about becoming owners, but for anyone interested in learning more about these extraordinary creatures. Find out what makes axolotls almost unique in the animal kingdom, how they never fully metamorphose (like other amphibians), and why they are sometimes called the Peter Pans of the animal world.

Introduction

Learn about the best aquariums for axolotls, what they eat - including the ideal diet for pet axolotls, and how to achieve and maintain the perfect water for an axolotl. This book will guide you through the best equipment, tank size, water plants, and everything else you need to keep a pet axolotl.

Learning about the challenges of caring for an axolotl, including detailed information about health issues, when to seek professional help, and helpful advice on how to treat minor problems at home.

Find out:

- How you can cool the water in an axolotl tank during warm weather.

- Why you might need to give your axolotl a tea bath.

- Where you should best place your axolotl's tank.

- When and how to 'cycle' the water in your aquarium (create your own nitrogen cycle).

- Which aquarium plants will create a great habitat for your axolotl; and those that could be harmful.

Discover the mythology associated with "Mexican walking fish," as axolotls are also known. Read about the Aztec god Xolotl, after whom axolotls are named, and how he cried so hard that his eyes fell out!

Understand how axolotls are helping medical researchers to find new ways to treat - or potentially cure - some of the most devastating and life-threatening diseases. Learn how wild axolotls have become among the most critically endangered

Introduction

creatures in the world, and how conservationists are working with scientists, farmers, and universities to help save wild axolotls from being lost forever.

And finally, why not try the fun and interesting activities, designed for anyone who loves axolotls, as well as activities for axolotl owners? Or test yourself with our axolotl fun facts and quizzes! Watch out for the very, very hard one!

So, read on & learn about these curious Mexican salamanders with their cheery smiles and fascinating biology - that with the help of the internet, have won over the hearts and minds of kids and adults from all over the world!

What Makes Axolotls So Cool?

Axolotls are so cool because they are so unusual. They look like little sea monsters, or perhaps fun-size aliens from another galaxy, or even friendly elfin creatures straight out of fantasy fiction. And it isn't just their appearance that makes them amazing - they have special powers that most superheroes would envy!

Axolotls are actually a type of salamander, a lizard-like amphibian found all over the world. There are approximately 760 species of salamander, some of which are common, such as the fire salamander, which is found throughout Europe, and the dusky and tiger salamanders, which can be found in swamps and along creeks in the United States. Some are much rarer, such as the critically endangered giant Chinese salamander, sometimes known as the "living fossil," and the world's largest amphibian, which can grow to 1.8 meters (5.9 feet) in length.

What Makes Axolotls So Cool?

Salamanders are fascinating creatures, with each species having its own wonderful and special qualities. But the strange little axolotl has gained a special place in the hearts and minds of people everywhere.

The axolotl is native exclusively to a particular area of Mexico, specifically the Lake Xochimilco and its surrounding waterways, located 28 km (just over 17 miles) south of Mexico City. There, these little "walking fish" (as they are also known, although they are not fish) have lived for thousands of years at the bottom of the sheltered shallows.

However, the axolotls found in most aquariums, pet stores, and social media posts are as different from wild axolotls as domestic dogs are from wolves. They are the result of decades of breeding; in fact, almost all pet axolotls, and those being used in science, are direct descendants of 33 axolotls that were captured by a German naturalist and explorer, Alexander von Humboldt, in 1863.

When these live specimens arrived at the Jardin des Plantes in Paris, zoologist Auguste Duméril was delighted. He managed to keep them alive, and by 1866, he had managed to breed embryos from seven of them. His research was continued by another German naturalist, Marie Von Chauvin, who made advances in understanding the axolotl's ability to metamorphose under certain conditions. The celebrated naturalist Charles Darwin included several paragraphs about the axolotl in his "On the Origin of Species" and suggested that it had evolved from a prehistoric amphibian, Ichthyostega.

They can grow up to 30 cm (12 inches) in length and weigh between 125 and 180 grams (4.4-6.3 ounces) when fully grown, with females being heavier than males. They have plump bodies with a dorsal fin that runs down their backs, and an eel-like tail. Their legs are short, with three fingers on their hind legs and four on their forelegs. The axolotl head is the widest part of its body, with feathery gills on each side. Its eyes are large, wide-set, and without eyelids; under a pair of tiny nostrils, it has a wide mouth that naturally appears to be happily smiling all the time.

The axolotl is covered in a slime coat, which is actually its mucous membrane that helps it glide through the water, like many other fish and water creatures. This slime coat also helps protect it from wounds, injuries, and parasites.

The Life Cycle of an Axolotl

The life cycle of amphibians - and salamanders - generally begins with the female of the species laying eggs in clumps. She will lay anywhere between 50 and 1,500 eggs, underwater, in dense areas of underwater vegetation, and after ten to fourteen days, the eggs hatch into tadpoles. In the wild, the hatchling survival rate is approximately 30-40 percent, with many being eaten by predatory fish.

Like all salamander tadpoles, axolotl hatchlings have external gills, tiny, blunt teeth in their upper and lower jaws, and eyes without lids. They swim at the bottom of the lake, much faster than adult axolotls. As they grow from this larval stage, they develop two pairs of legs and internal organs, including lungs, whereas other amphibians then develop further into newts, frogs, toads, or salamanders. The axolotl does not undergo metamorphosis in the same way, although it continues to grow and develop.

The axolotl breeds while it is still in this "juvenile" state, which is quite remarkable and very rare in the animal kingdom. In 1885, anatomist Julius Kollmann described this feature, retaining the juvenile state throughout its life, as neoteny. This term has been used to describe axolotls and a handful of other creatures that remain in what naturalists consider to be a juvenile state throughout their lives.

In rare cases, axolotls can develop beyond being an amphibian, Peter Pan, and will undergo the final change in the salamander lifecycle to metamorphose into a salamander. As an adult salamander, it will lose its slime coat, and from then on it will live on land (although this will usually be marshy grassland). This will only happen if they are exposed to certain hormones, or their environment changes drastically and they no longer have access to water.

Despite having lungs similar to those of frogs, toads, and other salamanders, and also being able to breathe through their skin, axolotls remain water creatures and use their feathery gills for breathing.

Superpower

The really magical, special superpower of the axolotl is its ability to regenerate itself. Some creatures can regenerate their limbs or tails when they are lost through injury, such as starfish, amphibious salamanders, and lizards. However, the regenerative ability of axolotls goes much further. In addition to being able to grow a perfect replacement limb without any scarring, they can also regrow missing eyes and other organs, including the brain and its spinal cord. The axolotl and the sea cucumber are the only living species known to be able to regenerate in this way. Because of this remarkable ability, axolotls are sometimes mistakenly believed to be immortal. This is not the case; axolotls generally live for five or six years in the wild, but much longer in captivity, where they can expect to reach the age of twelve; the oldest axolotl is thought to have celebrated its 22nd birthday.

Different Types of Axolotls

Most wild axolotls are brown, olive green, or black, with shiny, golden speckles called iridophores on their skin that help them blend in with their muddy underwater habitat. Their eyes are black but ringed with gold, and their frilly gills are purple or grey. They are usually darker in color than captive axolotls, and they are considered to be more robust and hardy than captive axolotls. Captive wild-type axolotls are usually called wild-type or olive axolotls.

The leucistic axolotl is much rarer in the wild. Leucism is the lack of some melanin, which is the natural pigment that gives skin (or feathers, or fur in other animals) its color. This axolotl type has dark eyes and pale, sometimes patchy or freckled skin, which is usually a pale, rosy pink or light yellow colour. Their gills are coral pink or red.

Albino axolotls are similar to leucistic axolotls, but they have no melanin in their bodies. There are two albino types: a white variety similar to the leucistic axolotl, but with clear or red eyes and without freckles, and the golden albino, which can range from a peach colour to an orange gold, although most are a gleaming bright yellow. They may have shiny patches on their skin, pinkish-yellow gills, and pale eyes. As babies, they are completely white, and it is almost impossible to distinguish them from albino hatchlings, but their yellow color begins to develop as they grow.

Speckled axolotls, sometimes called dirty leucistics, are pale colored but with a sprinkling of dark spots (called melanophores) on their faces, and sometimes on their bodies. As they age, these axolotls may develop many more spots.

Melanoid, or black axolotls, are very similar to the wild-type axolotls, but they do not have the iridophores - golden flecks - on their skin. They are completely inky black, with a lighter belly, and their gills are also very dark. They have no shiny patches on their skin, and they don't have gold colored rings around their eyes. A heavily marked melanoid axolotl is very similar to the black melanoid, but it has black dots on its skin that can be difficult to make out if it has dark skin. Some have brown or khaki dots, which are far easier to see.

There is also a melanoid golden albino axolotl, which is typically a cream or white color with yellow freckle markings. Because they are melanoid, they do not have sparkly iridophores.

The chimera axolotl, which has a left side that is a completely different color from its right, is very rare indeed. This happens completely naturally when two axolotl eggs are laid together, then fuse and grow as a single animal. The survival rate for chimera hatchlings is very low, and when they do grow, one side of a chimera axolotl can grow more slowly than its other side.

Mosaic axolotls are formed in a similar way to chimera axolotls, but the two colors are not evenly split on either side of the animal. Instead, two different colored varieties create a dappled area of color along the creature's back. Mosaic and chimera axolotls are often infertile.

Sometimes mistaken for a mosaic axolotl is the piebald axolotl. They are usually white or pale pink with patches of another color, which can be black, grey, olive, or golden. Breeders prize these axolotls because their colouring is genetic (unlike that of chimaera and mosaic axolotls), which helps them experiment with new patterns or colours.

Specially bred Axolotls

Other axolotl colours have been genetically modified by humans or created through embryonic grafting, and they only occur in axolotls bred in captivity, originating from the seven breeding axolotls captured by Alexander von Humboldt. Only one of these was a leucistic axolotl, and it is the direct ancestor of most of these beautiful domestic varieties.

The GFP (Green Fluorescent Protein) axolotl was originally bred by scientists to help in cancer research. The GFP gene that they introduced can be passed down generations of axolotls as they breed, so wild-type, leucistic, albino, or melanoid axolotls can be born with this gene.

Whatever its color, a GFP axolotl will glow a luminous green under ultraviolet or blue light, and if this wasn't amazing enough, some have the most beautiful, emerald eyes.

The firefly axolotl generally has a dark-colored head and a bright, fluorescent tail, which really does look a bit like a firefly, although it does not glow in the dark.

Copper axolotls are a special albino type that range from an attractive pale coppery color to a deep bronze. They have brown freckles, golden iridophores, and red-tinted eyes. Their bellies are often paler, sometimes with a pink tint.

The lavender axolotl is a rarer hybrid, and as its name suggests, has a purple-colored body covered with grey spots, and grey, pink-tipped gills. Its eyes are black. Some lavender axolotls will turn grey or green when they are fully grown.

The silver dalmatian axolotl is almost indistinguishable from the lavender axolotl. It is a pale, gleaming grey, dappled with little grey spots, and with the same black eyes. These lavender and silver dalmatian types have been bred from lighter melanoid axolotls.

Enigma axolotls are almost exclusively found in the United States. They are incredibly beautiful, and each is considered unique in the patterns on its skin. They can be golden, white, black, or olive with spots, stripes, splodges, or patches. Some breeders have even managed to create enigmas with multicolored gills.

The rarest and most desirable axolotl is the blue axolotl, but this is still not yet the true color in reality. Pictures of blue axolotls are often deceptive, having been manipulated with filters, and some owners have even managed to light their tanks to give their axolotls the illusion of having blue skin.

Some breeders are not just interested in the colors of axolotls; the RDG (Ridiculously Long Gills) have frilly gills that are so long, the axolotls cannot hold them upright.

Because captive axolotls are almost all descended from the Paris axolotls, there has been a lot of inbreeding, which is closely related to axolotls, as they parent babies together. This has had an impact on the genetic makeup of these axolotls-their genetic similarity is 35%, almost three times the ideal, which has resulted in certain health weaknesses in the species.

Cousins and Distant Relatives

As well as axolotls, there are several other species of neotenic salamanders (that is, salamanders that remain in a juvenile state and live in water).

A very close relative is the achoque, or Pátzcuaro salamander, which is only found in Lake Pátzcuaro, the third-largest lake in Mexico, approximately 300 km (200 miles) from the Xochimilca waterways.

The achoque once thrived in the lake; local fishermen caught 20 tons of these salamanders every year, but since the 1980s, this number has sharply decreased, and now there are barely any achoque left in the lake.

However, nuns at the Sisters of Immaculate Health Dominican convent, in the town of Pátzcuaro, stepped in almost thirty years ago.

The nuns had been making a special medicine they called Jarebe for 150 years and sold it to help people with respiratory problems. This cough syrup, so popular that its sales have been the main source of income for the convent, contains an ingredient extracted from the achoque's skin. When the nuns explained to a visiting friar (who was also a biologist) that the animal was becoming more difficult to get hold of, he persuaded them to start breeding achoques.

The nuns have two rooms filled with aquariums, and their breeding program has been extremely successful within these rooms. When scientists at the Michoacan University discovered how the convent was expertly breeding achoques that were dangerously close to extinction, they reached out and (with funding from Chester Zoo in the United Kingdom) extended the program. In addition to breeding the rare salamanders, the nuns now collect DNA samples and microchip them. The long-term aim is to release convent-raised achoques back into Lake Pátzcuaro, but there is a lot of work to be done in restoring their habitat and tackling pollutants in the water before that can happen.

There is another neotenic salamander with frilly gills that resembles the axolotl, which was discovered in 1984. This Anderson's salamander has only been found in Laguna de Zacupu, a much smaller lake than Pátzcuaro, in the state of Michoacán, Mexico.

In Lake Lerma, by the high-altitude city of Toluca, lives the Lerma salamander. Although it does look very similar to the wild axolotl, some of these salamanders do not remain in their neotenic state and develop functional lungs, making their lives in the grasslands surrounding the lake.

Mudpuppies, or water dogs, commonly found throughout North America, are also neotenic, although not classified as mole salamanders, like axolotls and the other neotenic Mexican lake salamanders.

Strange distant cousins

There are other unusual species of neotenic salamanders that are able to regrow damaged limbs.

This includes seven species of siren salamanders, each of which bears a strong resemblance to axolotls, albeit stretched-out, elongated versions. They are very long, like eels, are aquatic, and can grow up to a meter in length. They have frilly, external gills like an axolotl, but they do not work quite as well in this species, and sirens are forced to often take gulps of air from the surface (far more frequently than the axolotl).

In 2020, the neotenic ezo salamander was rediscovered in Lake Kuttata, located on the northernmost island in Japan. A few of these rare salamanders, like the axolotl, do not metamorphose. They had first been found there in 1924, but were declared extinct a few years later.

Perhaps the strangest neotenic amphibian that resembles the axolotl is the olm, found far, far from Mexico, in Europe. It lives in the waters of cold, underground pools that have formed in caves and tunnels along the Adriatic coast.

The olm has a long, skinny body, two pairs of tiny limbs, and feathery, pink gills on either side of its head, growing to about 30 cm (12 inches) in length. It is ghostly pale as it has no pigment in its skin. Although young olms have tiny eyes, the adults do not, which gives their faces a weird, spooky expression - no features, just a snout.

There is very little food available to them in their dark, underwater habitat. When they do sense a tasty worm or insect larvae, they eat huge amounts and are able to survive on such a meal for a long time - sometimes up to ten years - without eating again. Because of this, they conserve energy by hardly moving at all. They live for a very long time, some reaching their hundredth birthdays.

In previous centuries, when they were more common, local people sometimes came across them after heavy rain washed them from their caves. They were often called "human fish" because their pale, pink-colored skin looked similar to theirs; other people thought they might be baby dragons!

The olm is classed as "vulnerable," with an estimated 400 individual olms living in the wild.

A subspecies of the black olm was discovered near Crnomelj, Slovenia, in 1986. This dark-colored olm has a shorter body than the pale olm, a longer tail, and small eyes. It is thought to inhabit an area smaller than 100 square meters.

Axolotls in Science

Since the first axolotls arrived in Paris in the 19th century, scientists have been fascinated by these strange creatures. As they are quite easy to breed in a laboratory, they have been studied all over the world.

In the decades that followed the arrival of the von Humboldt axolotls at the Jardin des Plantes, biologists soon discovered that by keeping axolotls in an aquarium that was tilted and filled with plants and gravel to mimic the shore of a lake, the axolotls inside would metamorphose into salamanders if the water was gradually reduced, a little each day.

Medical researchers have been working with axolotls for many years, hoping to unlock the secrets of how they can regenerate and regrow their limbs and organs. If they are able to discover exactly how these genetic triggers work, there is an exciting possibility that humans or other animals could eventually repair their bodies in the same way - growing new tissue without scarring. Regenerative treatment like this could make a massive difference to people who have suffered terrible accidents, helping to heal wounds or conditions in which doctors have had to remove an arm, a leg, or another organ.

As part of their research, scientists working in Vienna, Dresden, and Heidelberg in Europe were the first to map the axolotl genome (the genetic information of an organism that tells our bodies how to grow and function). It is a really massive genome, because of a huge percentage of repetitive DNA (deoxyribonucleic acid) content, and scientists are still unsure of the reason for this. At 32 billion base pairs, it is ten times larger than the human genome (3 billion pairs) and among the largest of all living creatures. The largest living creature to be sequenced is a South American lungfish, which has 91 billion base pairs, whereas the largest known genome is a New Caledonian fork fern, with 160 billion.

Scientists believe that the completed axolotl genome will make the possibility of regenerative medicine much more likely.

Researchers studying axolotls have also found possible medical breakthroughs after examining the axolotl's slime coat. This mucous membrane is extracted from the axolotl by scientists wearing sterile gloves and gently massaging the axolotls, so as not to harm them in any way. The mucous is then extracted from the gloves with sterile scraper instruments.

Within this mucus are antimicrobial peptides, which could provide medicine with an alternative to antibiotics. This could be very important as humans and other animals are becoming increasingly resistant to antibiotics, which means infections can be more difficult to treat. In experiments, axolotl antimicrobial peptides have already proven effective against some extremely harmful and antibiotic-resistant bacteria, such as methicillin-resistant Staphylococcus aureus, more commonly known as MRSA, which can cause life-threatening sepsis infections.

Some of the antimicrobial peptides extracted from axolotl slime coat have been found to possess anti-carcinogenic properties, indicating that they may prevent or delay the formation of cancer cells. Early controlled biological tests on breast cancer cells have been really encouraging, and medical researchers are hoping this could help them develop new ways to treat this terrible disease in the future.

ACTIVITY #1

Color-in these axolotls so the colours you choose correctly fit the titles. You can design your own axolotl too, if you like...

A Wild Axolotl

What Makes Axolotls So Cool?

A GFP Axolotl

Leucistic Axolotl

What Makes Axolotls So Cool?

Albino Axolotl

Axolotl Facts for Kids

Color Your Own Axolotl!

What Makes Axolotls So Cool?

Piebald Axolotl

Activity #2

Why not draw the life cycle of an axolotl? You could do this as a diagram, or a picture, or maybe a cartoon strip! We left a blank page for you to get drawing!

Draw the Life Cycle of an Axolotl!

Axolotl Behavior and Communication

THE AXOLOTL IS KNOWN FOR ITS LACK OF ACTIVITY! IT SPENDS HOURS apparently immobile, gazing into the distance with its enigmatic smile like an amphibian Mona Lisa.

They often sit, completely still, for hours at a time, at the very bottom of their underwater habitat, especially as they get older. There they like to hide, sometimes burrowing into loose water vegetation, mud, or finding a small cave or hole in which to hide.

In the dark waters of Mexico's Xochimilco, axolotls have little need to hide, as they were the top of the food chain, the apex predator, until the introduction of some invasive species. However, this is simply how they are - motionless for long periods. Some experts even suggest that axolotls are the sharks of the Xochimilco - or at least they were before other species were introduced to those waters by humans.

Hiding away is very important to them; people who keep captive axolotls often find their pets will suffer from stress if they do not have hiding areas in their aquariums. They are nocturnal creatures, generally more active at night, and they prefer a dark or low-light environment. With their poor eyesight, bright, direct light can feel very uncomfortable.

In the wild, the axolotl spends much of its time hunting. Once it has seen or sensed its prey, it carefully finds the best position to attack. It then opens its mouth and expands its throat, which quickly decreases the pressure inside the cavity inside its body, and so it can powerfully suck the mollusc, worm, or little fish inside, trapping it inside.

As well as using its visual cues (its sight) and chemical cues (its sense of smell) for hunting, it will also detect electrical fields that are generated from the smallest movements of its prey. This is extremely helpful to the axolotl, as its eyesight is poor and the water in its natural habitat is often dark and murky. As a result, the axolotl is a surprisingly efficient hunter, perfectly equipped for the conditions in which it lives.

Despite their preference for benthic living (benthic is the term for plants and animals that live at the bottom of a water habitat), and breathing through their external gills, from time-to-time axolotls swim up to the surface of the water to gulp air into their lungs; a process known as "buccal pumping" that is fairly common among amphibians.

Although they are capable of moving through the water relatively quickly - perhaps up to ten miles an hour when faced with a threat - axolotls tend to swim slowly and purposefully, or potter along the ground, moving their legs to propel themselves. For this reason, the axolotl is sometimes known as the Mexican walking fish.

It is extremely sensitive to temperature, and as the water cools, its movements will become even slower.

Because they prefer a solitary life, axolotls have little need to communicate with one another. When they do, animal behaviourists believe they use lateral line organs along the sides of their head and body that help them recognise certain chemicals released in the water, allowing them to "smell" one another. This helps them "smell" food too.

Despite their poor eyesight, axolotls are thought to be able to recognize shapes from a distance. In the case of pet axolotls, they may recognize their owners, particularly if they have regular feeding times, and they might even be able to identify other family members or pets.

Some studies have suggested that salamanders are extremely intelligent. In a 2003 report, it was suggested that axolotls have the ability to count to at least three. Many owners have reported that their axolotls respond to them, even displaying affection or enjoying music.

Axolotls are considered to be adults when they are around six months old. Then, sometime between March and June, when the waters of the Xochimilco are more temperate, they are ready to breed.

Then, the male axolotl will stray from their territory to find a mate. When it finds a female who is ready to breed, the two creatures perform a ritual by which they twirl around together, in a circular motion, rather like they are dancing a waltz. During this dance, the male drops a cone-shaped mass of sperm from his cloaca (the chamber in an amphibian's body used for reproduction and digestion). The female axolotl then collects it with her cloaca, and this will fertilize her eggs.

After carefully laying each egg individually on rocks and waterweed, the female axolotl's role as a mother is over. She does not care for her eggs or the hatchlings when they emerge. In fact, she will probably eat them if they swim her way!

The eggs are a dark brown color (or white if the mother axolotl is an albino axolotl), and they are covered in a protective jelly coating.

After two or three days, the fertilized eggs will "bean," which means the embryo is developing, and the shape of the egg will gradually change from a round dot to a longer, oval shape. From then on, it continues to lengthen, and by the sixth day, it begins to curl, so it looks a bit like a comma. It is quite possible to work out which end will be the baby axolotl's head and which will be its tail at this stage.

Four or five days later, the embryo's gills are visible, and it has begun to resemble a small axolotl. Then, in the final days before it is ready to hatch, its eyes will become more prominent, and some of its markings might even be detectable.

In the period immediately before hatching, the embryo will start to twitch, but when it finally hatches, it will seem to fall to the bottom of its environment and will barely move. This is because it does not need to feed for a day or so, as its stomach still contains some of the egg yolk that nourished it as an embryo.

Axolotl larvae are born with all of their organs, so over the first weeks and months of their lives, they will increase in size (around an inch per month) and grow their four legs. Although axolotls do not have a natural predator in their native underwater environment in the Xochimilco waterways, the youngsters are indeed very vulnerable. With native crayfish, aquatic birds, snakes, and fish feeding on them, as well as adult axolotls, the hatchling survival rate is low, probably around 30-40 per cent.

This is a serious problem for axolotls in the wild today, as the population has dwindled to an estimated 1,000, and its future depends on the survival of its eggs and larvae.

Activity #1

What do you think axolotls are thinking about while they sit, gazing into space? Fill in the thought bubbles on the next page with your ideas...

Axolotl Facts for Kids

Axolotl Behavior and Communication

ACTIVITY #2 (for axolotl owners)

Do you think your axolotl is intelligent? Does it recognize you or family members?

OBSERVE your pet closely and set up a table in a notebook or on your smartphone, tablet, or computer to record any behavior you think demonstrates this. Make sure you make a note of feeding times and regular events in your household that your axolotl might be reacting to.

What do Axolotls Eat?

AXOLOTLS WILL EAT ALMOST ANYTHING THAT FITS IN THEIR MOUTHS. Because of the way they suck food into their mouths and throats, they have little control over what they swallow along with their prey.

Although carnivorous (i.e., an animal that eats meat), they often consume algae, small pieces of waterweed, gravel, and water in the wild.

Despite having tiny teeth, they do not bite, tear, or chew their food; instead, they suck it into their mouths and digest it whole. Their tongue is a flat pad, fixed to the lower part of their mouths (for those rare axolotls that metamorphose into a salamander, this tongue will be replaced with a long tongue they can stretch out to catch insects, like many other amphibians). Despite this, they have approximately 1,400 taste buds, allowing them to enjoy - or not enjoy - whatever they are eating. Wild axolotls are not considered picky eaters.

Biologist and ecologist Dr. Luis Zambrano has examined the gut contents of wild axolotls, clarifying what these animals eat in their natural habitat. Surprisingly, since the creature is carnivorous, algae and plant matter made up twenty per cent of the matter he found inside. Chironomids (non-biting midges) accounted for 30 percent; small fish, 10 percent; soft-bodied invertebrates (such as worms), just 5 percent; and digested mollusc shells (snails), another 10 percent. Small crustaceans and other invertebrates made up 16 percent, and the remaining 9 percent of the gut matter he extracted was also composed of crustaceans, specifically ostracods - tiny seed shrimp. Even though these axolotls had consumed a lot of plant matter, it does not provide much nutritional benefit to the axolotl.

Fortunately, for owners of pet axolotls, feeding their pets a healthy diet is not quite as complicated, but there are several different ideas about the best way to do this.

A worm diet

Most breeders and experts agree that worms, which are high in protein, are a good staple diet for their axolotls and recommend red wigglers or European night crawlers. Both of these are compost worms that are easy to find, to farm, or inexpensive to buy.

Some owners believe that pet axolotls should be fed exclusively on this type of worm, with only occasional treats to vary their diet. The amount they should be fed is not an exact science, but at all ages, a feeding session should be between three and five minutes, and a healthy axolotl should eat as much food as it wants within that time.

When feeding a worm to an axolotl, it will need to be cut to the correct size, so it can easily fit inside the axolotl's mouth. Then, the worm morsel can be dropped over its head, so the axolotl can sense it and gulp it up. However, if the axolotl doesn't catch the worm, it will fall to the bottom of the tank, and it may well remain there since an axolotl's instincts are to catch live food. For this reason, many prefer the tweezers method by which the feeder offers the axolotl its wormy lunch using aquarium tongs or long tweezers. It is best to try to "wiggle" it a bit, and then the axolotl should quickly show interest and gobble it up. If it misses, and the worm falls to the bottom, it is easy to pick it up with the tongs, ready to try again.

Sometimes axolotls may regurgitate larger, uncut worms - especially live worms - and it is thought that this could be due to the worm's movement irritating the axolotl's stomach. If an axolotl does regurgitate food, it is always possible that it has rejected it because there is something wrong with it. It is never a good idea to try giving that same morsel to the animal again.

A pellet diet

Another option is to feed pet axolotls with pellets that have been specifically manufactured to suit their dietary needs. These can be very convenient, especially for squeamish owners who are not very happy about cutting up live worms, and they are designed to sink so that the axolotl can find them. Owners should choose a high-quality pellet, designed exclusively for the axolotl, and the right size for their pet (they are generally available in several sizes). Depending on the variety and the individual axolotl's needs, they will generally eat somewhere between five and ten pellets per feeding session.

The disadvantage of pellet feeding is that it can cause constipation in the axolotl, and, of course, it is not a natural food and may contain additives. Pellet-fed axolotls will often learn to forage at the bottom of the tank for their food, but any uneaten pellets need to be removed from the tank before they begin to break down and dirty the water. A high-quality pellet can be a great choice if worms are not available, or to keep as an emergency meal replacement.

Although pellets are generally dropped over the axolotl's head during feeding time, allowing it to gulp them as they fall, some enterprising owners have introduced feeding dishes for their pets and enjoy watching them dine like cats and dogs. Very cute.

Treats and Side Orders

As well as pellets and compost worms, owners preferring to give their axolotls a more varied diet will often introduce bloodworms, which can quickly become a favorite. Still, they are unsuitable for the axolotl's main diet because they are high in fat. Ghost shrimp, red cherry shrimp, and brine shrimp (also known as sea monkeys) can also make tasty treats for axolotls.

Other supplementary foods should be properly prepared before being fed to an axolotl. Raw salmon and tuna are often very popular, but they must be frozen, thawed, or flash-frozen as sashimi to ensure it doesn't contain parasites.

Owners who like to feed small fish to their axolotls must be very careful, as sharp bones can pierce their pet's soft mouth or throat. This also applies to some invertebrates. Pet axolotls seem less able to digest chitin - a substance found in the outer skeleton of insects and crustaceans - than their adult wild cousins. However, too much chitin does cause the death of a large proportion of baby wild axolotls in Mexico that have not reached adulthood.

Much more controversial is feeding axolotls on beef heart, pet dog food, or the occasional pinky (baby mice). Although many axolotls that have tasted these morsels are reported to have loved them, it is unnatural for them to eat mammal meat of any kind, and most experts and breeders consider it a very bad idea.

Feeding a Growing Axolotl

By the time they are fully grown, axolotls should be fed once a day, once every other day, or even every three days in some cases. It really depends on that individual animal, but owners soon grow used to their axolotl's needs. The amount of food they require can also vary, but most experts recommend feeding them as much as they choose to eat in a three-minute (or so) feeding session.

Baby axolotls grow very quickly - an inch (2.5 cm) per month for their first six to eight months - and need to be fed far more often. Daphnia (common water fleas) is a firm favorite with most axolotl breeders. Although the high fat content and lack of other nutrients make bloodworms unsuitable as a regular food for adult axolotls, they are an ideal meal for fast-growing, hungry little ones. Baby axolotls will need feeding several times a day.

In fact, hungry little axolotls are always hungry and are well known for their unfortunate tendency to nibble on their siblings if given the chance, so it is advisable for owners to separate youngsters as soon as possible.

Once young axolotls grow to around 10 cm (4 inches), their feeding times should be reduced to twice a day, and then to once a day when they are six months old and have reached their full size. A good rule of thumb for axolotl owners is to regularly inspect their pet from above - a healthy animal's head should be the same width as its body. If it looks to be gaining too much weight, the owner should either reduce the amount of food they are giving their pet, or the frequency of its mealtimes.

And it should also be noted that axolotls should never, ever be fed buckets of tropical fish - unless, of course, they are Minecraft axolotls!

ACTIVITY #1

Design a menu for an imaginary axolotl café! Maybe you can find a way to describe pellets, worms, and other axolotl treats so that they sound more inviting!

ACTIVITY #2 (for axolotl owners)

Why not make your own worm farm? As well as growing a plentiful supply of axolotl food for your pet, seeing how worms make rotting vegetation into compost is fascinating and will give you a great understanding of their importance in the natural world. You can buy kits or learn how to construct them online.

Caring for Your Pet Axolotl

THE MOST IMPORTANT RESEARCH FOR ANYONE WANTING TO KEEP AN axolotl is to ensure it is legal to keep axolotls in their state or country, and to determine whether there are any restrictions on owning an axolotl. In most countries, axolotls can only be purchased if they have been bred locally and cannot be imported from other countries.

It is currently illegal to keep axolotls as pets in California, New Jersey, Virginia, and Maine in the United States. Additionally, anyone living in Hawaii and New Mexico must obtain a permit before keeping an axolotl. Pet axolotls are banned in New Brunswick, British Columbia, and Prince Edward Island in Canada, and there are restrictions in Nova Scotia. This is not always because they are a critically endangered species, as some might imagine, but because they are classed as a non-native species that could pose an environmental threat to struggling native species (such as Eastern tiger salamanders and California tiger salamanders) if they were released into the wild. In Europe, it is illegal to sell any kind of animal that has been genetically modified, which may restrict the variety of axolotls available.

A large part of caring for a pet axolotl is understanding its environment and its needs. Before handling an aquarium or anything that will be placed inside, it is very important for that person to clean their hands thoroughly with hot water, without using soap or any other chemicals, such as sanitizing gel or detergents, and then dry them with a paper towel. Even a clean towel could leave traces of fabric cleaning residues on the cleanest hands.

Creating the Ideal Environment

Axolotls need plenty of space and plenty of water, so most experts recommend an aquarium of at least 110 liters (29 gallons), whatever the size of the axolotl. It is important to choose a tank that is wide rather than tall, as axolotls like to amble along the bottom from time to time and swim from side to side. Although they are not known for their curiosity and climbing ability, axolotls have been known to escape from an aquarium lid, or a net covering is a very good idea.

The tank should be positioned well away from direct sunlight; a cool basement is ideal if possible, and it should be kept away from household appliances such as televisions and refrigerators.

Before placing axolotls in an aquarium, even if it is brand new, it should be thoroughly cleaned with hot water to remove any bacteria that might harm its new inhabitants. Then, it should be filled with water treated with a de-chlorinator, which will remove chlorine, chloramine, and other metals that might be harmful to the axolotl. Then, the equipment can be added.

Thermometers

An essential piece of an axolotl care kit is a thermometer. It is extremely important to maintain a cool temperature in an axolotl tank, ideally between 15°C and 18°C (60-65°F). If the temperature becomes too warm, it can cause the axolotl to suffer physically and shorten its lifespan. Conversely, if the water becomes too cold, the axolotl will become cold, anxious, and may stop eating. You can read more about this in Chapter 5, "Keeping Axolotls Healthy."

Using a thermometer is the only way to be certain of the water temperature in the tank, but there are three different types of thermometers to choose from. The first is a simple analog thermometer, which has probes that should be positioned just below the rim of the water, inside the tank. A tube of red alcohol will then mark the temperature on the scale. Some of these aquarium thermometers are marked with a "safe" area, which axolotl owners should ignore, as this is a guide for people keeping tropical fish. Despite being "low tech," these analog thermometers are generally considered very reliable and give accurate readings. They are less expensive and serve as a good backup for individuals who prefer other types of thermometers.

Another option is a digital display thermometer that is submerged inside the tank. Although it is very easy to read, many owners report finding them worryingly inaccurate. Therefore, for axolotl owners considering a digital display, it is sensible to have an analog thermometer as a backup, allowing them to verify the accuracy of the reading.

The third option is the extremely reliable but expensive laser thermometer, a handheld "temperature gun" that is aimed at the aquarium water (never at the glass) to give a truly accurate reading. It is certainly worth the investment for individuals who own multiple aquariums.

Fans and Coolers

During the summer months, it can be difficult to keep the axolotl's water cool. Air conditioning can be extremely helpful, and some owners prefer to buy portable units - especially those living in warmer climates.

Clip-on fans are a great way to cool the water temperature in a tank, although some models are more effective than others. They blow cold air across the surface and can really make a difference, reducing the temperature by several degrees in some cases. Because these fans evaporate water, it is important to keep an eye on the tank's water level and to regularly top it up (with dechlorinated water) when the level drops.

Water chillers are expensive but very effective and require a pump or canister filter. Beginners often find them challenging to set up, but experts at aquarium suppliers can provide helpful advice.

During very hot spells, axolotl tanks can be cooled much more cheaply by taking several plastic water bottles, filling them with dechlorinated water, and putting them in the freezer for several hours. Once frozen, one can be submerged in the water in the aquarium, and it should bring the temperature down. More can be added if the water is still too warm, and as they defrost, they should be removed and replaced with new, frozen bottles. It is important that these bottles are clean before being used as chillers for the axolotls.

Filters

As well as a thermometer, axolotl aquariums need a low-level filter to remove some of the waste particles from the water. The low-level mechanism will not create too much interference with the movement of the water in the aquarium, which is much better for axolotls.

There are two main types of filters. A canister filter is positioned outside the tank. It draws water through a tube and pumps it through biological, chemical, or mechanical media, which removes dirt particles, then it releases the clean water back into the tank. It is a good idea for anyone thinking of keeping an axolotl to discuss how they might best filter their tank with an expert at a specialist aquarium store.

A sponge filter uses a sponge as the mechanical media to trap the dirt as it flows through. They are generally inexpensive, easy to clean, and powered by an air pump or power head.

As well as cleaning the water, which is good for the axolotl's health, having clear water is much better for the owners. Having clear, pristine water helps them observe their pet and understand its behavior, which is really important for any responsible owner.

Light and dark

Some owners like to add lights to their aquariums. Some amphibians can benefit from UVB lighting, which helps them produce vitamin D3, vital for building healthy bones. However, it is widely considered that axolotls have no need for it and certainly prefer a dark, murky atmosphere in the wild. Ideally, only low-level lights that cover just up to a third of the tank should be added to an axolotl aquarium that contains plenty of plants, and these lights should always be turned off at night.

Axolotls love to have dark places to hide in their aquariums. There should always be a few hidey-holes or gloomy caves for them to enjoy. Experts recommend using twisted pieces of natural bark, ceramic pieces specifically designed for aquariums, or even pieces of drainpipe.

Cycling

Once the aquarium has its filter, accessories, and has been filled with dechlorinated water, it is ready for cycling. This is very important for the health of an axolotl and can be quite a complicated procedure. It is the process of creating a nitrogen cycle, to break down axolotl waste (mainly its pee and poop), which releases ammonia into the water, and is harmful to the pet.

Cycling encourages beneficial bacteria to form in the filter, which will "eat" ammonia particles. After about a week, the ammonia levels in the water will begin to drop, indicating that friendly bacteria have started to form. These bacteria release nitrite, which is also toxic to axolotls. However, as the nitrate levels increase, a second bacterium forms, which consumes these nitrites, causing the aquarium's nitrite levels to also begin to decline.

At this phase of the cycle, when nitrate levels have started to increase, some of the water needs to be changed. Most owners recommend a 25-50% water change every week. Water-changing systems, like the Python No Spill Clean and Fill, make this job a lot easier. Any water being added to the tank must be treated with a de-chlorinator.

At the beginning of the cycling process, it is essential to test the water daily using a testing kit. Test strips are quick and easy to use; they are dipped into the water in the tank and change color according to the amount of chemicals they detect in the water. Then the strip can be compared with a color card guide.

However, strip tests are not as accurate as chemical testing kits, which contain several tubes or containers. A sample of the aquarium water is tested with different chemicals that will change color according to the amount of ammonia, nitrites, and nitrate present in the water. This process can be a bit daunting to begin with, but it is a much more accurate method for testing the water and understanding the nitrogen cycle.

The perfect readings for the water in an axolotl tank should be:

Ammonia: 0 ppm (parts per million)

Nitrites: 0 ppm

Nitrates: 0-10ppm

pH: 7,4-7,8

General water hardness (GH): 7-14°

Carbonate hardness: (KH): 3-8°

Oxygen saturation: 70-100%

Salinity: Salt is not required; however, 20-40% Holtfreter's or John's solutions are recommended (more information on this topic can be found in Chapter 5, "Keeping Axolotls Healthy").

A new aquarium should be tested every day. Once the readings have stabilized and are within the right parameters for an axolotl, weekly testing is generally enough.

It is essential that the cycle is working before an axolotl is introduced to the tank, and there are several ways to help start this process. Specialist pet stores can help explain further and give advice about the best products and systems for cycling an aquarium.

Introducing an axolotl to an aquarium

Once the aquarium is ready for its axolotl, the animal has to be acclimatized - made ready for its new home. The easiest way to do this is to place the axolotl in a plastic freezer bag filled with half water from the tank. Once the bag is secured with a band, it can be gently placed inside the tank for fifteen minutes. Then, the owner should make a small hole in the bag, and the axolotl remains inside it for another thirty minutes. Only then should the bag be opened and the axolotl, which by then is used to the water, be released into the tank.

A lot of owners like to add a substrate (a natural surface at the bottom of the tank). Gravel is a poor choice as axolotls can occasionally mistake it for food. Far better is a fine sand, or pebbles that are larger than the axolotl's head.

Water Plants

There is little doubt that axolotls love to share their homes with plenty of plants, which also help to oxygenate the water and absorb small amounts of ammonia and nitrates, which helps to maintain great water quality. However, some plants can be toxic to axolotls, so it is important to check before adding a plant to the aquarium. Small, floating plants, although not toxic, might be mistaken for food and ingested by an axolotl from time to time, potentially proving harmful to the animal.

Before any plants are added to an aquarium, they need a chemical dip treatment to get rid of any eggs or organisms that might be attached or hiding in the foliage, which could affect the axolotl living there.

Suitable stem plants include water wisteria, guppy grass, hornwort, and Rosanervig. Rhizome plants and mosses that thrive in low-level lighting include Java moss, Marimo moss balls (provided the balls are larger than the axolotl's head), weeping moss, and varieties of Anubias.

Rooted plants need loose substrate upon which to anchor themselves. Axolotl-friendly species include tiger Vallisneria and several varieties of Echinodorus, such as the tiger and yellow sun varieties.

Several varieties of floating plants are also suitable, but they may need to be corralled (kept within a smaller area). Water lettuce, duckweed, and red root floater are popular choices.

Some axolotls share their tanks with non-aquatic plants. It is quite possible to grow several popular houseplants, with their roots in the water and their foliage above. Silver dollar maidenhair fern, peace lilies, and varieties of fittonias can look very attractive, but the plant should be properly rooted in a separate container of water before it is added to the tank.

It is never a good idea to add plant fertilizers to the water in an axolotl tank, as salamanders have semi-permeable skin and might absorb harmful substances.

All About Poop

Axolotl poop is usually brown or black, about 2.5 cm (an inch) long, and weighs about a gram (0.04 ounces). It "arrives" in a very thin membrane, a bit like a sausage skin, but if it isn't promptly removed from the tank, it will dissolve into the water.

The poop can be scooped up, or some owners prefer to use a Turkey blaster to suck it up and remove it.

Unfortunately, axolotl poop contains ammonia, which is very harmful to the animal (see Chapter 5, Keeping Axolotls Healthy), so owners need to be very careful while removing this poop, so the membrane doesn't break. Ammonia is also toxic to humans, so disposable gloves should always be worn for this unpleasant task. In any case, axolotl poop can smell really horrible! The good news is that an adult axolotl will generally poop about once a week.

If an axolotl doesn't seem to have pooped, the owner should check the levels of ammonia and other chemicals in the water straight away, as it is most likely that they have missed a poop and it has dissolved into the water. However, if they are certain the axolotl has not pooped, or if it looks bloated, they should speak to a veterinarian.

Axolotls do not eat their own poop, so if an owner notices their pet has been doing this, it is a sign that all is not well, and again, a specialist veterinarian will be able to help or treat the axolotl if it is sick.

Young axolotls that eat more will poop more, and their poop is just like that of an adult, but smaller and lighter. It is just as important to remove it from the aquarium, so cleaning a tank of axolotl poop is a much more time-consuming job until an axolotl becomes an adult.

Tank Mates

As far as tank mates are concerned, axolotls are solitary creatures and prefer to live alone. For owners who simply can't bear to see their pets living all alone, small shrimp can be introduced, or some fish with similar needs to axolotls, such as guppies, danios, and certain snails, but they will need to keep an eye on them since fish often like to nip at an axolotl's feathery gills.

Anyone considering keeping more than one axolotl in the same aquarium should invest in a much larger tank; experts recommend 340 liters (90 gallons) or even larger. Some owners are sure their axolotls are much happier living with a friend (or two). In contrast, others feel just as certain that it is of no benefit to keep axolotls together unless the intention is for them to breed, and due to the numerous problems that have arisen from inbreeding axolotls, this is something best left to experts.

~

ACTIVITY #1

Draw the best possible aquarium for an axolotl. Remember to give it plenty of nice, dark hiding holes and lots of plant life for it to enjoy. (Use the next page if you need more space!)

ACTIVITY #2 (for axolotl owners)

Make a schedule to help you care for your axolotl. You can log your water temperature, water quality, the frequency of water changes, and any observations you make.

Keeping Axolotls Healthy

For anyone who keeps an axolotl, ensuring a good quality of water in its aquarium is vital for its health and wellbeing. Many ailments suffered by these extraordinary amphibians are caused by poor tank maintenance, specifically failing to keep up with the nitrogen cycle and maintaining the correct water temperature in their aquarium. This is why it is crucial to check the tank's water quality weekly, perform regular water changes, and maintain a water temperature between 15°C and 18°C (60-68°F) in the tank.

A healthy axolotl should be plump, not fat, with fluffy gills and no damage to its skin. However, most new owners will find it difficult to spot many health problems. For this reason, it is always a good idea for a specialist amphibian or exotic pets veterinarian to check over a new axolotl pet as soon as possible. They should notice any concerns and will often screen the axolotl for parasites with a fecal test. Thereafter, a yearly check-up at the veterinary surgery will help to keep an axolotl in tip-top condition.

Although most pet axolotls do not tend to suffer from poor health, there are diseases and ailments their owners need to be aware of, some of which can be treated at home. However, it is always best to get advice from a veterinarian or an aquarium expert.

There are several signs that an axolotl may be sick or highly stressed. For example, some axolotls may start to swim frantically, a behaviour that is very unusual in the species. In this case, the owner should check the aquarium filter's flow before consulting a veterinarian, as a strong current may have caused the axolotl to react in this way. If it is a filter issue, the axolotl needs to be checked regularly after this has been addressed, as any stress it has endured due to the damage to its environment could affect its health.

Lots of axolotls spend a great deal of time floating in the water. However, an axolotl floating upside down is a cause for concern, and a veterinarian should be contacted because its buoyancy has likely been affected, probably due to excessive air ingestion, which requires medical treatment. It is normal for axolotls to take in small amounts of air, which is perfectly healthy. Sometimes, they will even "toot" a few little air bubbles from their rear ends.

Another indicator that the axolotl might be unwell is a curled tail - even if it's just the tip. As soon as an owner notices this, they should test the water parameters immediately. If the issue is not related to the water, they should contact a veterinarian for advice.

Chemical Contamination

Often, the first sign that an axolotl is sick is changes to its feathery gills. Suppose they appear to have deteriorated or started curling outward toward their face. In that case, it is essential to test the aquarium water immediately, as this can be a symptom of high ammonia levels or chemical contamination. Some axolotls will use their hind legs to try to scratch at their gills, much like a dog with fleas, and this is a particularly telling sign that they are experiencing some discomfort.

Chemical contamination can be frightening and, if left unchecked, can be very harmful to the axolotl; however, it is usually caused by commonplace household products, such as soap, cleaning products, and perfumes. If this has occurred, the axolotl needs to be removed from the tank. If another aquarium is not available, the axolotl can be placed in a large tub of dechlorinated water inside a refrigerator. This is a comfortable, safe environment where it can stay until the tank has been thoroughly cleaned with hot water, then refilled. Unfortunately, this will have disrupted the nitrogen cycle, so the aquarium will then need to be cycled from the start all over again.

Some owners prefer to buy aquarium remedies to treat the water. But it is crucial to verify exactly what is in these compounds, as some substances that are harmless to fish can be toxic to axolotls. These include anything containing malachite green, copper, or magnesium, so it is always sensible to check with an expert before use.

If the ammonia levels in an aquarium are left to rise, an axolotl can suffer badly. It is likely to swim to the top of the tank to take in large gulps of air, and its gills may become red and inflamed, appearing severely damaged. In an aquarium with very high ammonia concentrations, the axolotl will develop bright red areas on its skin - these are chemical burns.

This is extremely painful for the axolotl, and it could prove fatal. As soon as an owner realizes their axolotl has been burnt in this way, they need to take action quickly. A second aquarium, or large tub, should be carefully cleaned with hot water (without soap or detergent) to ensure it does not contain traces of any substance that might worsen the axolotl's condition. It should then be filled with clean, dechlorinated water that is cooler than the water in the axolotl's existing tank.

The axolotl can then be placed in the refrigerator or cooled with bottles of frozen water. During this time, the water in the container should be changed twice a day.

Meanwhile, the aquarium and all of its contents, including the filter, should be thoroughly cleaned. The cycling process will have ended and will need to be re-established, with much more regular water quality checks.

An axolotl exposed to high nitrate levels for too long might irritate the delicate tissues around its eyes and cause it to develop "bulging eye disease." If left untreated, the axolotl could lose its sight; therefore, it is essential to consult a veterinarian for treatment.

Bacterial and Fungal Infections

Poor water quality or infected food (especially if it has exceeded its "use by" date) can result in an axolotl developing bacterial infections. If this is the case, the animal will eat very little, if at all, and suffer from gill deterioration. Other symptoms could include reddened skin, ulcers, and bloating. If it is left untreated, it is unlikely to recover, so it is important that it is seen by a veterinarian as soon as possible so it can be treated with antibiotics (usually by medicine for it to swallow, or an injection).

Aeromonas hydrophila is a bacterial disease commonly known as "red leg" that affects amphibians, particularly in overcrowded tanks or poorly maintained water. It is carried in the animal's blood, a common complaint among captive axolotls. An axolotl that contracts this disease will develop red patches on their feet and other areas of its body. Although veterinary attention is important, owners can start to treat their axolotls with 100% Holfreter's solution - a balanced salt treatment that tackles bacterial infections in amphibians. It is important to mix this solution with hard water when treating axolotls (other amphibians prefer soft water).

Another treatment to consider is Nitrofura-G, an antibiotic medication designed exclusively for axolotl care. It is easy to use, with very clear instructions, but it is very important to be certain that the axolotl is suffering from a bacterial infection before thinking about using this product.

Fungal infections are among the most common problems in axolotl aquariums. Generally, this is easy to recognize, as the animal's gills, legs, or head develop clusters of cloudy white fuzz, and minor cases are easily treatable. They should not seriously harm the axolotl if it is caught early.

Some owners prefer to use a black tea bath to help treat their axolotls if they notice this type of infection. A cup of organic, caffeinated black tea, in which a teabag has been steeped for fifteen minutes and then completely cooled (with the bag removed), is added to a tub filled with 4 liters (1 gallon) of dechlorinated water. The axolotl is then placed in this tea bath for ten minutes, allowing the anti-fungal tannins in the tea to address the infection while the axolotl relaxes. This treatment is then repeated daily until the infection has cleared. More serious or persistent fungal problems will need stronger medication, possibly a hydrogen peroxide application, which a specialist veterinarian can recommend.

There is a particularly nasty bacterial infection called columnaris that can be mistaken for a fungal infection, as an affected axolotl will develop white or grey patches of bacteria that resemble a fungal infection. This disease could prove fatal if left unchecked, but it is relatively easy to cure if caught early (treatments include a stronger concentration of Holfreter's solution or regular salt baths). To ensure the sick axolotl receives the correct treatment, it is always best to seek the advice of an expert or specialist veterinarian, since salt solutions can be very harmful to axolotls. Unnecessary exposure to saltwater for long periods can result in serious gill damage.

Some owners suggest adding a few drops of an antiseptic/disinfectant, such as Mercurochrome, that can be bought from a pharmacy to the water of an aquarium to help treat axolotls with minor bacterial or fungal infections; expert Peter W. Scott recommends 2-4 grams ppm (parts per million) to a thousand liters (264 gallons) of water, which will tint the water a slightly orange color.

There are other compounds that can treat fungal infections in axolotls, most of which contain a medication called methylene blue, which is safe for treating axolotls. Furazolidone, an antimicrosporidal, is sometimes used to treat fungal infections and some parasitic infestations. But, of course, it is very, very important to carefully follow every instruction when using chemicals near animals, and it is always best to consult a veterinarian.

Wounds, Cuts, and Grazes

Axolotls suffering from wounds, such as the loss of a leg or fin damage, will usually heal themselves so long as the wound does not become infected. A wounded axolotl should always be separated from any tank mates. Many owners prefer to use 100% Holfreter's solution as a preventative measure, as it helps reduce levels of harmful bacteria in the water that could cause an infection in the wound.

While it is healing, it is advisable to feed the axolotl as normal, but to cool the aquarium slightly, so it remains at 15°C (60°F). Axolotls seem to recover more quickly at lower water temperatures.

It is also important for owners to keep a close eye on any damage to an axolotl's slime coat. Since it serves as a protective barrier against bacterial and fungal infections, as well as some parasites, and helps the axolotl regulate its temperature, any lesions could lead to health problems for the animal. If the water parameters in an aquarium are good, damage to its slime coat should heal quite quickly.

Again, it is a good idea to cool the water temperature, and some experts suggest adding Indian almond leaves to the water, claiming it can boost the axolotl's immunity. These leaves slowly release tannin into the water, which can help stabilize water levels that have become slightly acidic.

Parasites

Like most animals, axolotls are vulnerable to parasites. Internal parasites, which prefer to live inside the axolotl, such as certain single-cell protozoa, can cause the axolotl to experience problems with its slime coating; 100% Holfreter's solution can be very helpful, though some experts recommend using a glacial acetic acid solution, or even vinegar, to get rid of them.

Some axolotls may become infested with roundworms, which they likely picked up from the live food they have eaten. This may explain the worrying weight loss and general sluggishness in the animal. A veterinarian might recommend a levamisole injection treatment or a deworming medication to be added to the axolotl's meals.

External parasites, which attach themselves to an axolotl's skin or gills (such as free-living flatworms), can be treated with magnesium sulphate, which should rid the aquarium of these unpleasant and unwanted visitors.

When treating axolotls for parasites (or other ailments), owners often choose to move their axolotls to a "hospital" container, where they can keep a close eye on their pet. It is essential to clean everything in the aquarium and replace the water carefully, as some parasites can survive in the water for a long time. There is little point in treating an axolotl only for it to pick up more unwanted passengers when it returns to its home.

Health Problems and Diet

Of course, food and diet are very important to an axolotl's health. Some axolotls, that are not given enough to eat as youngsters, will stop growing. These "minis" can be as small as 15 cm (6 inches) and are likely to have other health issues.

Impaction is another name for digestive blockages, usually due to the axolotl swallowing an oversized item of food or something indigestible, such as a piece of gravel. In some cases, this can prove fatal if left unchecked, so it is vital that an owner seek medical help if their axolotl is suffering this way.

In the meantime, the axolotl should not be fed and should be kept as cool as possible to help it pass the blockage.

As with feeding any pet, a poor diet will ultimately cause problems for the animal. For example, an axolotl given a diet low in calcium may develop MBD (metabolic bone disease) and experience difficulties moving due to the softness of its limb bones. This can be remedied to some extent with an improved diet of calcium-rich earthworms.

Fluid retention can also be an effect of a diet with too much oil or fat - this was especially true during a period when some owners were persuaded that it was a good idea to feed their axolotls on pet food intended for dogs.

When caring for an axolotl, owners must take a responsible attitude toward their food. With a pet that is often inactive, it can be very tempting to give it extra food and treats. However, axolotls, like most animals, are vulnerable to obesity if they are overfed. Unsurprisingly, this is a common problem, and it can seriously shorten an axolotl's life.

Other Health Problems

There are some genetic abnormalities that can become apparent in young axolotls as they grow. Often, these cannot be treated. If the axolotl has heart or kidney problems, fluid may build up in its body. Some veterinarians are prepared to drain this fluid with a hypodermic needle, but often prefer not to, as it will often build up again.

Unfortunately, some axolotls suffer from genetic disorders that are often the result of poor breeding.

Axolotl hatchlings and embryos that are affected by genetic disorders. Larvae suffering from twisted gills cannot feed and will die within a couple of weeks. Lethal homozygous is another condition, in which the gills are fragile and curl inward, and most larvae will not survive. Similarly, most hatchlings born with the stasis gene, which causes them to have bright red livers and develop anemia, will die very quickly. Other young axolotls may develop temporary anemia as they grow, but most recover as they become adults. Cardiac non-function, which affects a hatchling's heart, is also lethal.

Some larvae may carry the pinhead gene, which affects their eyes, the front of their brains, and their mouths. Only a few mildly affected hatchlings will survive. Microphthalmic larvae, which develop very small eyes, will also die within days of hatching.

Vasodilation is caused by a recessive gene that lowers the blood pressure of a larva after hatching. The few that survive to adulthood with this condition are much smaller than their siblings.

Short toes are a mutation that affects the axolotl's kidneys, female reproductive organs, and its limbs. It can be diagnosed by its short limbs and a strange, coiling swimming pattern, and unfortunately, these axolotls will not survive more than twelve months. There is another genetic mutation in which larvae grow as normal until they are at the stage when they should develop digits on their limbs, but these are deformed, and the larva will die soon after.

Some axolotls can be born without eyes, but with careful hand feeding, can live quite happily in captivity. However, it is very important that other axolotls are kept in the tank.

When caring for an axolotl, it is really important to have access to a good veterinarian who specializes in amputations or exotic pets. It is also very helpful to have the support of experts in axolotl care at an aquarium center who will offer advice on how to keep your pet in tip-top condition for a long and healthy life.

∼

ACTIVITY #1

Find out ways in which we can help support axolotls in the wild. There are numerous nonprofit organizations and wildlife charities running awareness campaigns to help us understand axolotls and the threats they face.

ACTIVITY #2 (for axolotl owners)

Add regular health checks to your axolotl care schedule. Observe your axolotl's behavior every day, looking for signs of illness. Check for changes to your pet's gills, skin color, or appetite. Make sure you contact your vet if you notice any serious symptoms.

Axolotls in Legends and Stories

Aztec Mythology

In the 16th century, Bernardino de Sahagún, a Spanish Franciscan friar (a monk from the Roman Catholic religious order formed by St Francis of Assisi 300 years before), was a missionary in South America. He devoted himself to converting the people of colonial New Spain (now Mexico) to Christianity, believing that the best way to do so was to understand the beliefs, culture, and history of those who lived there.

He learnt Nahuatl, the Aztec language spoken by the people of Central Mexico. He set about recording everything they could tell him in twelve books, which he called La Historia General de las Cosas de Neuva España ("The General History of the Things of New Spain"). It is a remarkable study, written in Nahuatl and Spanish, with more than 2,000 illustrations hand-painted by local artists.

Bernardino de Sahagún's Florentine Codex, as it has become known, contains two illustrations of axolotls and mentions them twenty times. It describes the axolotl as looking like a lizard, "...it has legs, it has a tail, a wide tail. It is large-mouthed, bearded. It is glistening, well-fleshed..." in Book 11. Unfortunately (for axolotls), it continues its description as, "... not very bony, good, fine, edible, savory." The Nahuatl people very much regarded the axolotl as dinner.

There is, however, a telling of the myth of the god Xolotl (after whom the animal is named).

Xolotl was the twin of the feathered serpent god Quetzalcoatl, and whereas Quetzalcoatl was golden and glorious, Xolotl was monstrous and misshapen - often portrayed with the head of a dog. He is the god of fire, lightning, death, and twins. In Aztec mythology, he accompanied his twin to the underworld to collect the bones of the dead, in order to create humans in the story of the Five Suns, and is often said to guide the dead on their journey to Mictlán, the "place of the dead."

The most well-known story of Xolotl (which was written of in the Codex) is in the legend of Teotihuacan, the ancient city. After the creation of the fifth sun, the gods were worried that it did not move in the sky. They decided each of them should be sacrificed to persuade the sun to move, and the wind god Ehecatl began to kill them.

Xolotl was frightened and didn't want to sacrifice himself. After crying so hard, his eyes fell out, leaving their sockets empty.

He then made his escape. First, he transformed himself into a maize plant with two stems and hid in a field of green maize, but he was soon discovered. Then, he changed himself into a double maguey plant, but again, Ehecatl found him.

Finally, he metamorphosed into an axolotl and dived into the water, where he thought he would be safe, but the wind god caught him and killed him.

Despite his (and the other gods') sacrifice, the sun still did not move until the wind forced it to walk, followed by the moon.

Almost all of the other axolotl references in the Codex are about hunting them and eating them. Apparently, they made a very good stew and, when roasted, were best served with maize.

They were eaten in a dish prepared with yellow chilies during the annual Izcalli festival, an important Aztec celebration of growth and rebirth dedicated to Huehueteotl/Xiuhtecuhtli, their ancient god of fire. As a part of the "fun," Aztec children were encouraged to catch axolotls and other small creatures, and then throw them into the burning fires in their homes.

Art and Literature

Perhaps because axolotls are only found in central Mexico (and the Jardin des Plantes in Paris since the 19th century), they have not been greatly celebrated in the arts outside until more recent times.

In 1956, the Argentinian writer, Julio Cortázar, published a short story with the title "Axolotl." It was about a man who visited a captive axolotl in Paris and became completely obsessed. He describes its "eyes of gold," its "rosy little body," and its gills as "three tiny sprigs, red as coral…" Eventually, the man in the book develops such a bond with the animal that he himself metamorphoses into an axolotl.

Other Mexican writers such as Gutierrez Tibón, Juan José Arreola (who has described the axolotl as a "...small lizard of jelly. A large water worm with a smooth flat tail and ears of coral ..." in his 1964 book Confabularto and Other Inventions), and Salvador Elizondo - who has recounted the Xolotl myth with hand drawn illustrations, have marveled at the salamander native only to their country.

Mexican poet, José Emilio Pacheco who wrote of the axolotl being, "...neither fish nor salamander, neither toad nor lizard, he has human features ..." and wondered about its strange existence, something that also fascinated the celebrated Mexican poet Octavio Paz, and sociologist Roger Bartra who thought that the axolotl could be seen as a symbol of Mexico, a country he suggested has never fully matured.

Roger Bartra is also the author of an anthology, "Axolotiada, Vida y Mito de un Anfibio Mexicano" (Axolotliada, Life and Myth of a Mexican Amphibian), in which he collected the history of the axolotl and the art and literature associated with it.

The Mexican painter, Diego Rivera, best remembered for his wonderful, colorful murals, included several axolotls surrounding the male and female figures in his 1951 mural "Water, the Origin of Life" on the Cárcamo de Dolores hydraulic works in Mexico City. This part of the artwork was supposed to be underwater but after just two years, the paint began to show signs of deterioration after just two years. There have been many restoration projects to save "Water, the Origin of Life," which is now a museum.

Ulf Rollof, a Swedish artist, developed a fascination with axolotls, and he produced Project Axolotl, a strange installation using light and water in which he explores the connection between axolotls and humans.

Film and Television

Elena Sakayan, a biologist and filmmaker, made a short film about a young woman's relationship with some axolotls in an aquarium in 1981. She gave it the title, "Who will Awaken the Axolotl?" and it is a strange and unsettling piece that asks questions about evolution, both in the axolotl and in humans.

More recently, in 2022, "Cenote", an award-winning animated movie, was released. It is the story of Axel, a young axolotl who gets separated from his family and magically transported to an underwater sinkhole. He befriends Memo, a human, to help him return home. Toothless, the Night Fury Dragon from the movie "How to Train Your Dragon," is said to be partly based on an axolotl. A lot of owners have seen such a resemblance between their pets and the character that they couldn't help but name their axolotl "Toothless."

Axolotls have featured in many nature and animal programs for children and young people. Dora the Explorer and her friends helped a baby axolotl find its way home, and the Octonauts have had an adventure, in which Captain Barnacles and Kwazii meet a pair of performing axolotls.

In Disney's Gravity Falls, the axolotl cosmic being, which exists between time and space, is a powerful being. Known as "the Frilly Know It All" and "the Frilly Guy Upstairs," it is central to many of the stories.

Disney has also developed axolotl characters in its Amphibia series. Efty, Gertie, and Leopold Loggle - all axolotls - all help Anne, the main character, return to the human world.

Axolotls in Legends and Stories

In the Mexican American animated television series Onyx Equinox, based on Aztec, Maya, and Zapotec mythology, the god Xolotl is introduced as an axolotl, having been transformed into a salamander by his twin brother, the god Quetzalcoatl.

Games

In 1985, Nissin, a Japanese food company, began using a cute axolotl as a mascot for a range of UFO yakisoba instant noodles and introduced a series of television adverts. These featured real pink albino axolotls, as well as a funny cartoon version, and the public quickly fell in love with these strange animals. Before then, axolotls were relatively unknown in the country, but it wasn't long before everyone seemed to be singing axolotl songs and buying Axolotl merchandise.

In fact, axolotls have become such an integral part of Japanese culture that Ghost wire: Tokyo, a horror adventure game in which the player is tasked with freeing the city from evil spirits, collecting items from Japanese myths, legends and culture to help them, a model axolotl is one of these relics ("Treasure 73").

Given Japan's love of axolotls, it is hardly surprising that a blue water-type Pokémon called Wooper is based on an axolotl. The Japanese word for an axolotl is uparupa, often anglicized to "whooper looper," which seems to suit the Japanese kawaii (cute) aesthetic perfectly. It is certainly a great improvement on its former name in the same language, *ahorōtoru*, which sounded a lot like the Japanese for "stupid old person"!

Wooper (who was introduced in Pokémon Gold and Silver) has a flat tail, three stripes decorating its body, and pink antennas rather than gills on the side of its head. It does not have front legs or the happy little smile that real axolotls are so well known for. Wooper is very popular in the Pokémon community because it can beat entire games on its own, and many players really like the way it looks. In Pokémon Scarlet and Violet, a black and brown variant called Paldean Wooper was added to the Pokémon world. Wooper, unlike real axolotls, will eventually evolve to metamorphose into Pokémon Quagsire.

Tamagotchi has two iconic characters based on axolotls. The first is an adult-stage character called Axolopatchi, who is pink with a plump little body and even pinker, frilly gills. Axolopatchi is "very lively, cheerful, and fun to hang out with," a description that doesn't really fit a genuine axolotl!

The second Tamagotchi axolotl character is Woopatchi, who is white with rainbow gills. She also has a cute curl on her head, and a lovely pair of pink lips! She is a virtual pet in several Tamagotchi games and can wear several fun accessories. Cogimyun Woopatchi and Meduupa also have some features based on axolotls.

Even cheerier than Axolopatchi (and even further removed from the personality of the quiet, reserved Mexican salamander in the wild) is Dr. Shrunk, the axolotl comedian in Animal Crossing. With glasses, large teeth, and square gills, he has been a character in almost all the Animal Crossing variations. He teaches players special emotions to use while playing with other characters online. In Animal Crossing: New Leaf, he is the owner of Club LOL.

Axie Infinity, a strategy video game that was developed in Vietnam and released in 2018, invites players to collect, breed, and battle digital pets that are based on axolotls.

Axolotls in Legends and Stories

Minecraft is the best-selling video game of all time, with over 300 million copies sold. It was developed and published by the Swedish video game developer, Mojang Studios, and released to the public in 2011. It has two strands: creative mode and survival, that can be played on various platforms, including smartphones, tablets, and consoles, and axolotls are extremely popular in both.

In Minecraft Survival, players who find axolotls can tame them to hunt for fish to help them survive. Even though they cannot defend players against mobs or fight against them, they are very popular - probably because they are so cute. In Creative Mode, players can build amazing structures and aquariums for their virtual axolotls.

Internet

Axolotls have also captured the imagination of YouTube content creators, who have made impressive cartoons and shows about all aspects of these fascinating creatures.

TikTok and Instagram craze of drawing funny faces on the glass of their aquarium, immediately in front of their pet, to make it look as though their pet has great hair, a cute hat, glasses, or even an impressive curly moustache and beard.

Some inventive owners have also added googly eyes to make their axolotls look funny, or have drawn detailed pictures, added stickers, and other bits and pieces to make their axolotls look like characters such as Harry Potter in Hogwarts, Captain Jack from Pirates of the Caribbean, or even President Trump!

The ridiculously catchy axolotl song, "There's an axolotl on the pink stair," has featured in thousands of social media posts. It has been animated, enacted by real and toy axolotls, and its lyrics humorously rewritten by exasperated parents who cannot get all of its verses out of their heads!

There have been several internet posts and stories in which AI (artificial intelligence) has been used to try to fool the axolotl-loving public. For example, generated photographs of axolotls supposedly caught by Papuan fishermen appear to be as large as a fully grown man. There are similar pictures of massive axolotls said to be found by the shores of Limbe in Cameroon. Another is "Bubbles," the AI-generated "sweetest giant axolotl ever," who is so large, he can barely fit into a bathtub!

Social media, such as TikTok and Instagram, have hundreds of thousands of posts about axolotls. Within minutes of scrolling, users are told how they can draw axolotls, crochet axolotls, bake axolotl-themed cupcakes, and build axolotls with construction bricks.

There are quizzes to see what color you would be if you were an axolotl, or whether your spirit animal might be an axolotl, and even to find out if it is possible that you are the "reincarnation" of an axolotl!

There is axolotl artwork, tattoos, cupcakes, and nail art to admire, as well as photos of axolotls in zoos, aquariums, and in the wild. Almost every conceivable aspect of axolotls can be found within a few clicks or a bit of scrolling.

And, of course, there are manufacturers and retailers ready to sell a mind-boggling array of axolotl products such as toys, stickers, stress balls, t-shirts, phone cases and charms, stationery, and even onesies.

Axolotls are now a massive part of youth pop culture, and their popularity shows no sign of coming to an end.

ACTIVITY #1

Why not write your own story or poem about axolotls? You could retell the story of the God, Xolotl, or imagine what it must be like to be an axolotl in the wild - or in captivity.

Activity #2

Perhaps you could try making an axolotl animation. It could be just a flip book, making an axolotl walk across the river bed or swim along the page, or perhaps you could have a go at a stop motion (or stop frame) or digital animation!

Axolotls in the Wild Today

Although axolotls have thrived in captivity, their wild cousins are dangerously close to disappearing altogether.

The number of axolotls in the wild dropped from 6,000 per square kilometer (15,509 per square mile) in late 1998 to an estimated 100 per square kilometer (260 per square mile) in 2015 - a really concerning decrease of 98 percent within ten years. And since then, the number of axolotls in the wild has continued to decrease.

This is because of a number of factors, including the illegal fishing trade, pollution, and invasive species being introduced to the Xochimilco waterways.

Habitat

When the Aztecs settled in the Valley of Mexico in the early 14th century, they introduced chinampas - floating islands of farmland - to the shallow lakes, including almost all of Xochimilca, the lake where axolotls are found. These "islands" were, in fact, great rafts, covered with soil, upon which vegetables and flowers were grown with their roots able to draw water from the lake below.

This method of farming suited a lot of the local wildlife very well, and especially axolotls.

They became a regular dish for the Aztec people who lived in Mexico, tasting somewhat like the frogs' legs eaten in France, a bit like a cross between fish and chicken.

As well as eating them, the Aztecs used axolotls for medicine, rituals, and believed the strange salamanders had the power to make women pregnant if they bathed in the waters of Xochimilco.

The Aztec Empire ended after the Spanish conquest of Mexico in 1521. The Europeans quickly introduced their own methods of farming, and many of the chinampas were abandoned.

Biologist and ecologist Dr. Luis Zambrano, a leading axolotl expert, conducted an axolotl census in 2014 to determine the number of axolotls remaining in the Xochimilco ecosystem. He and his researchers entered the canals by boat, shot nets into the water, and counted the axolotls they found. As Dr. Zambrano had feared, the situation was very serious - they found fewer than 35 axolotls per square kilometer (91 per square mile). He believes there may well be no wild axolotls left in the large canals of Xochimilco, and that the tiny remaining axolotl population is making its home in the smaller waterways.

Why are Axolotls Endangered?

As well as the chinampas being abandoned, axolotls have suffered because of urban expansion and pollution in Mexico City, which has affected the oxygen levels of the waters of Xochimilco.

It is almost certain that the quiet, solitary wild axolotl population has been badly affected by the vibrant and colorful trajineras - party boats with bright lights, mariachi bands, great food, and dancing - that glide across the Xochimilco every evening. These boats, which resemble Italian gondolas, have been an integral part of Mexican culture for centuries. In recent times, a fun-filled cruise along the river has become an unmissable part of the Mexico City experience.

And then in the 1960s, non-native fish species were introduced into the Mexican waterways as a source of food for the people. Unfortunately, tilapia and carp quickly discovered that axolotl eggs and tadpoles made a fine source of food for themselves. When they weren't eating baby axolotls, they ate the same worms, mollusks, and crustaceans that adult axolotls depended on for their survival.

A large number of chinampa farmers in Mexico had stopped using parts of their land for agriculture and had instead built football fields; providing a venue for players had proved more profitable than growing maize in a country where many are obsessed with "the beautiful game." The problem, especially for axolotls, is that to repurpose this land, the farmers have filled in the small waterways that separated the island farms.

The loss of these axolotl habitats has been such a concern that the UNAM has been working with these farmers to help them return their fields to farmland. Many have agreed to return to vegetable growing and reopen the smaller canals for the sake of the future of axolotls.

Abandoned Pets

Although axolotls have become regular superstars on internet sites and social media, and the public has taken their sweet little faces to their hearts, unfortunately, this has not been very beneficial to the species. Some of the people who have taken them in as pets have quickly become tired of their lack of activity, the need to constantly monitor the water quality in their tanks, and are frustrated by the amount of space an aquarium uses in their homes.

This is not a new phenomenon; Disney's Finding Nemo animated movie had a similar effect on clownfish in 2003, and the game Minecraft has had a similar impact on the axolotl.

Pet shelters have been swamped by axolotls, especially after owners have accidentally placed breeding pairs together in their aquariums. This often results in thousands of baby axolotls - and the nightmare of trying to find homes for them.

Some irresponsible owners, who have grown tired of their pets, have abandoned their axolotls. Enough of those that have survived this horrible experience have been found and rescued to make it clear that this is a problem. The pink albino type axolotls bred in captivity are particularly vulnerable in the wild, as they are the perfect prey for snakes and birds.

This is why it is so important for anyone considering becoming an axolotl owner to learn as much as they can about this commitment and to think carefully about it before bringing an axolotl into their home.

Restoring Axolotls' Habitat

After the alarming 2015 axolotl census, Dr. Zambrano and his research team realized a long-term plan would be needed to save wild axolotls from extinction. They understood the importance of having the support of local people, especially those who farm the land or make a living from fishing or sailing on the Xochimilco. With this in mind, a program to save axolotls was launched, called the National Chinampa Refugio project, which involves a return to the traditional Aztec farming method of chinampa farming.

The idea is for axolotls to inhabit the canals between the island plots, which are called refuges. Gates made from wooden frames and plastic nets prevent large, invasive tilapia and carp fish from entering these areas, and filters help prevent pollutants from spoiling the water in the refuges. Project workers testing it have found it to be of a much better quality, within the ideal temperature for axolotls, and without harmful chemicals.

The filters are made from a porous, volcanic rock commonly used in the building industry in Mexico. Called tezontle, it is full of holes in which beneficial bacteria can eat pollutants and sewage, just like a vast version of an aquarium filter.

In addition to these man-made filters, native aquatic plants such as bulrushes and broadleaf cattails, which have long been recognized as natural filters, form a kind of water hedge around each stand plot, allowing their roots to help draw unwanted chemicals from the axolotl refuge canals. On the shores, Bonpland willow trees and wooden stakes help to stabilise the land and prevent it from breaking, and pieces from falling into the water.

Within these refuges, full of good quality, filtered water, are other species such as acocils (small Mexican crayfish) and little fish called charales, both of which make up part of wild axolotls' diets. After they have been established, frogs and other wildlife that thrive in good quality water are soon spotted. The water becomes crystal clear, and this healthier ecosystem can act as a buffer zone against climate change.

The local farmers who have taken on the axolotl refuge chinampas grow native plants, herbs, vegetables, and fruit. They are forbidden from using any chemical pesticides or any fertilizers that might affect the water parameters or harm the axolotls. The food they grow is organic, of a really good quality, and far better than anything mass-produced in the supermarkets, so they can generally expect much higher prices at market.

In the past (which some elderly people can still recall), the chinampas measured 10 by 100 meters (33 by 330 feet). However, with the refuge canals, the size of each plot varies, and they are only accessible by canoe.

Fifteen years after the launch of Chinampa Refugio, the results have been encouraging. Forty refuge chinampas have been established; the aim is to scale up and eventually build more than 400 chinampa farms in Xochimilco with refuges for axolotls.

As part of the project, the National Autonomous University of Mexico (UNAM) launched a campaign inviting the public to pay for an island refuge, "adopt" a wild axolotl, or to "buy lunch" for an axolotl, depending on how much they chose to donate.

Fortunately for the axolotl, its fame has been a great help in the battle to save it from extinction. Many people who, before the 1980s, had never heard of these strange little creatures, have rallied to the cause, sending money to help preservation projects.

Attempts to restore axolotls to Xochimilco have not always been successful. On a very hot day in 2022, an attempt to release 200 axolotls into Xochimilco, with a great blaze of publicity, ended in embarrassment and worse for the animals themselves. Politicians involved in this publicity stunt were busy having their photographs taken and answering the media's questions. At the same time, the poor axolotls that were due to be released suffered badly in the glare of the hot sun for far too long, and most are believed to have died soon after.

However, in 2025, a report was published that is really good news for the future of axolotls in the wild. Eighteen axolotls, which had been bred in captivity by scientists, were fitted with radio transmitters so that they could be tracked. Then, eight were released into Xochimilco, and ten into man-made wetlands.

Twice every day thereafter, volunteers returned to the sites where the axolotls had been released to track their progress, and the results were surprising and very interesting. It proved captive-bred axolotls are able to return to the wild, which is unusual; most animals bred in captivity would not be able to survive.

The released axolotls explored a much larger area than the scientists expected before they settled in their new homes, and those in the man-made wetlands settled well. This is really encouraging for the future of the species. Of course, it would be far better to have a thriving population of wild axolotls in the Xochimilco River. Still, it is reassuring for conservationists to have a 'plan B' for the animal's future.

A museum and conservation center, Axolotitlán, dedicated to the axolotl, opened in Mexico City's Chapultepec Zoo in 2013. As well as being able to see four different wild species of axolotl, there is an exhibition hall, workshops for kids, and four laboratories in which axolotls and their environment are studied.

It is also home to "La Gorda" ("the chubby lady"), an axolotl who will live on forever in Mexico's history. Little Gorda is said to be the axolotl featured on the Banco de Mexico's 50-peso banknote, issued in 2021. It was an immediate sensation, so popular that online sellers were offering to sell it for 500,000 pesos! Although the banknote is in circulation, it appears that people are collecting it rather than spending it.

And La Gorda, though very beautiful indeed and the star attraction at Axolotitlàn, is not exactly the banknote axolotl; she was one of several images used by the artist who created the design.

∽

ACTIVITY #1

Make or design a poster to inform people how cruel it is to abandon unwanted axolotls. Perhaps your local aquatic pet store or veterinarian's surgery might put it on display?

Activity #2

Axolotls, like many animals, are at risk because of global warming and pollution. Make sure you play a part in helping the planet. Find out about ways that you can conserve water, save energy, and support wildlife. You might not be able to help wild axolotls, but there are lots you can do that might indirectly help their habitat.

Are You Ready to Own an Axolotl?

Quiz 1 - Are You Ready to Own an Axolotl?

Answer the following questions, with either "true" or "false," to help you decide whether an axolotl is the right pet for you.

1. I would like a pet that I can cuddle.
2. I am fascinated by amphibians.
3. I think it will be very easy to look after an axolotl.
4. I would like an aquarium full of axolotls, fish, and other sea creatures.
5. I would like a pet that is very active and fun to watch.
6. I would like an axolotl because I have seen how cute they are on social media posts.
7. I only have room for a tiny tank, but I would love to own an axolotl.

Axolotl Facts for Kids

8. I really hate creepy crawlies, and I would hate to see a pet eating a bug or a worm.
9. I am very interested in chemistry and biology, and I would like to create a fantastic, healthy environment for an axolotl.
10. I would like a pet that would help me get some fresh air and exercise.
11. I would like an axolotl, but it is illegal to keep them in the state where I live.
12. I have read 'Axolotl Facts', I understand how to look after them, and I feel sure I will be a responsible owner.

ANSWERS BELOW:

1. I would like a pet that I can cuddle.

IF YOU ANSWERED "TRUE", then an axolotl is not the pet for you. Axolotls should be handled as little as possible. Some experts recommend wearing clean, disposable nitrile gloves whenever you must pick up an axolotl.

1. I am fascinated by amphibians.

IF YOU ANSWERED "TRUE," then an axolotl might be a good pet for you. They are other amphibians you might want to consider, such as Pacman (or American horned) frogs, fire belly newts, or tiger salamanders (that have been bred in captivity as they are

Are You Ready to Own an Axolotl?

an endangered species), but axolotls are easy to care for if you set up an aquarium properly, cycle your tank, and commit yourself to spend time and effort ensuring the water is perfect for an axolotl.

1. I think it will be very easy to look after an axolotl.

THIS IS a bit of a trick question! Axolotls are generally easy to care for, provided the water in their aquarium is properly maintained through regular testing (at least weekly) and water changes.

1. I would like an aquarium full of axolotls, fish, and other sea creatures.

IF YOU ANSWERED "TRUE," then an axolotl may not be the best pet for you. Axolotls are not sea creatures; they live in freshwater environments, and they are solitary animals that are best kept on their own. It might be a good idea for you to think about keeping tropical fish or other exotic aquarium species instead.

1. I would like a pet that is very active and fun to watch.

IF YOU ANSWERED "TRUE," an axolotl might not be the best pet for you. Axolotls often remain completely still for long periods and tend to hide away. However, when they do march along the bottom of their tanks or take a little swim, they are fascinating to observe. So, if you are a very patient person, an axolotl might be the perfect pet!

Axolotl Facts for Kids

. . .

1. I would like an axolotl because I have seen how cute they are on social media posts.

IF YOU ANSWERED "TRUE," you should probably give owning an axolotl a lot more thought. There is nothing wrong with admiring other people's pets - especially if they are a bit unusual or exotic - but you really need to understand what is involved in properly caring for an axolotl (and the same goes for any other pet) before you commit to owning one.

1. I only have room for a tiny tank, but I would love to own an axolotl.

IF YOU ANSWERED "TRUE," then unfortunately, an axolotl is not for you - until you have a bit more space. Axolotls need a large tank - no less than 110 liters (29 gallons) - and natural biologists who have studied them are now of the opinion that an even larger environment would be better.

1. I really hate creepy crawlies, and I would hate to see a pet eating a bug or a worm.

IF YOU ANSWERED "TRUE", then an axolotl probably wouldn't be a good choice for you. They are carnivorous animals that need to be fed on worms (or slices of worm), shrimps, and other small water life. Although they can be fed on pellets, it is still a good idea to supplement an axolotl diet with the occasional worm, mollusk, or crustacean, which may be a bit too much for you!

Are You Ready to Own an Axolotl?

. . .

1. I am very interested in chemistry and biology, and I would like to create a fantastic, healthy environment for an axolotl.

IF YOU ANSWERED "TRUE," then an axolotl might be the perfect pet for you. The primary focus of caring for an axolotl is creating and maintaining a suitable, cycled environment, which is likely something that you will find very rewarding.

1. I would like a pet that would help me get some fresh air and exercise.

IF YOU ANSWERED "TRUE," then you really need to re-read this book and learn more about axolotls!

Unless you plan to visit your local pet store for supplies, owning an axolotl will not provide you with many opportunities to exercise.

1. I would like an axolotl, but it is illegal to keep them in the state where I live.

IF YOU ANSWERED "TRUE," then, unfortunately, you cannot keep an axolotl.

People who keep banned species could face legal action and the possibility of a hefty fine.

1. I have read "Axolotl Facts" I understand how to look after them, and I feel sure I will be a responsible owner.

IF YOU ANSWERED "TRUE", then it sounds like you are ready to own an axolotl! But, don't forget that owning any pet, although usually a source of great pleasure, is a major commitment, and that you are responsible for their welfare.

TRUE OR FALSE?

Some wild axolotls are found in the ocean.

The answer is False.

Wild axolotls are only found in the Xochimilco waterways in Mexico City.

Easy Axolotl Quiz

QUIZ 2 - AXOLOTLS, TEST YOUR KNOWLEDGE (MULTIPLE CHOICE)

Score one point for each correct answer!

WHAT DOES THE WORD "AXOLOTL" mean?

1. "River chicken"
2. "Blob fish"
3. "Water dog"
4. "Pond lizard"

2. In which country are axolotls found?

1. Mexico

2. Brazil
   3. The United States of America
   4. Canada

3. What creatures like to eat baby axolotls?

   1. Water birds
   2. Snakes
   3. Some fish, such as tilapia
   4. Bigger axolotls

4. What kind of habitat do wild axolotls prefer?

   1. Clean, clear water with a strong current
   2. A rock pool near a sandy beach
   3. The murky, shallow Xochimilco river bed
   4. A large aquarium with cool, cycled water, plenty of water plants, and places to hide, properly maintained by a responsible owner.

5. What color is an albino axolotl?

   1. Olive green
   2. Pale pink or white
   3. Copper
   4. It can be any color

Easy Axolotl Quiz

. . .

6. What do most axolotls like to eat?

    1. Sashimi salmon
    2. Blood worms
    3. Sea monkeys
    4. Night crawlers

7. How do axolotls socialize in the wild?

    1. They seem to be very competitive and like to race one another.
    2. They seem to be very sociable and like to live in large communities.
    3. They don't.
    4. They live in pairs and will remain together for their whole lives.

8. In which range of length is an average healthy adult axolotl?

    1. 5 to 10 cm (2-4 inches)
    2. 15 to 45 cm (6-18 inches)
    3. 60 to 75 cm (24-30 inches)
    4. 80 to 90 cm (32-36 inches)

9. What is the lifespan of a pet (captive) axolotl?

    1. 2 - 5 years
    2. 5 - 10 years
    3. 10 - 15 years
    4. 15 - 20 years

10. What status has the International Union for Conservation of Nature given to the axolotl?

    1. Critically endangered
    2. Vulnerable
    3. Near Threatened
    4. Least Concern

TRUE OR FALSE?

The axolotls' slime coat may help medical researchers find an alternative to antibiotics?

Go to the back of the book to find the answers!

The Hard Axolotl Quiz!

QUIZ 3 - AXOLOTLS, TEST YOUR KNOWLEDGE

The Really, Really Hard One!

1. What is the Latin name (binomial nomenclature) for the axolotl?

   1. Ailuropoda melanoleuca
   2. Ambystoma mexicanum
   3. Ceratotherium simum
   4. Panthera uncia

2. What are iridophores?

Axolotl Facts for Kids

   1. Amphibians that gulp their food using their mouths and throats to create a vacuum.
   2. Golden flecks are found on the skin of wild axolotls and some captive breeds.
   3. A type of small, freshwater shrimp that is a good source of protein for axolotls.
   4. Axolotls that continue to metamorphose into salamanders.

3. What does benthic describe?

   1. An animal with a slime coat.
   2. An animal that gulps its food using suction.
   3. An animal that prefers to live alone.
   4. An animal that lives at the bottom of a body of water.

4. What is the name of the Aztec underworld, with which the god Xolotl is associated?

   1. Mictlin
   2. Hades
   3. Valhalla
   4. Jigoku

5. Which of the following organs can an axolotl regrow?

The Hard Axolotl Quiz!

   1. Its brain
   2. Its tail
   3. Its spinal cord
   4. Its eyes

6. How many base pairs are in the axolotl genome?

   1. 2 billion
   2. 13 billion
   3. 23 billion
   4. 32 billion

7. Approximately how many species of salamander are there?

   1. 360
   2. 560
   3. 760
   4. 960

8. What are the filters in the National Chinampa Refugio project made from?

   1. Natural sponge
   2. Volcanic rock
   3. Recycled aluminum
   4. Rock salt

. . .

TRUE OR FALSE?

Charles Darwin suggested axolotls have evolved from prehistoric ichthyostega?

Go to the back of the book to find the answers!

The Fun Axolotl Quiz...

THE FUN QUIZ!

One point for each correct answer!

1. What is strange about Dr. Axolotl, the mad inventor in Disney's animated series, Tailspin?

   1. He can fly
   2. He is a vegetarian
   3. He is actually a lizard
   4. He can't swim

2. What is the collective noun for a group of axolotls?

Axolotl Facts for Kids

   1. An army
   2. A maelstrom
   3. A slumber
   4. A wandering

3. What is the name of the axolotl said to be featured on the Mexican 50 peso banknote?

   1. Melanie
   2. Big Betty
   3. La Gorda
   4. Alexis Pottle

4. Which Pokémon is based on an axolotl?

   1. Bulbasaur
   2. Eevee
   3. Lugia
   4. Wooper

5. According to the popular song, where might you find an axolotl?

   1. On the pink stairs
   2. On the lawn chair
   3. On the high street

The Fun Axolotl Quiz...

4. At the front door

6. What is the name of the largest recorded axolotl?

    1. Lottie
    2. Axel
    3. Frida
    4. Glob

7. What is the rarest axolotl in Minecraft?

    1. Golden axolotls
    2. Blue axolotls
    3. Rainbow axolotls
    4. Translucent axolotls

8. Why shouldn't you take an axolotl on vacation with you?

    1. It is almost impossible to find suitable holiday clothes for them.
    2. They are extremely picky about holiday destinations.
    3. It is extremely difficult to pack an aquarium.
    4. Because it will probably paxalotl!!

How many points did you score?

0 - 2: Axonotl!

3 - 4: Axolittle!

5 - 6: Axolotl!

7 and over: Axolotsandlotl!

True or False?

The GFP axolotl will glow a luminous pink under ultraviolet or blue light?

And now for a knock-knock joke....

Knock knock!

Who's there?

Axolotl.

Axolotl who?

....

Go to the back of the book to find the answers!

THE FINAL ACTIVITIES!

Activity #1

Try writing your own axolotl quiz, word search, or crossword. Don't forget to use lots of the facts you have learned from this book!

Activity #2

Why not have a go at creating an axolotl board game? Perhaps it could be a race to save them from extinction, or an adventure game based around an aquarium. Of course, it could just be something colorful, happy, and fun to celebrate your favorite smiley amphibian!

Answers: Easy Axolotl Quiz

QUIZ 2 - AXOLOTLS, TEST YOUR KNOWLEDGE (MULTIPLE CHOICE)

Score one point for each correct answer!

∼

WHAT DOES THE WORD "AXOLOTL" mean?

1. "River chicken"
2. "Blob fish"
3. "Water dog"
4. "Pond lizard"

The answer is 3.

The Nahuatl word for water is "atl," and the Aztec god Xolotl is often portrayed as a dog, so "axolotl" is a combination of the two, "water-dog".

. . .

Answers: Easy Axolotl Quiz

2. In which country are axolotls found?

   1. Mexico
   2. Brazil
   3. The United States of America
   4. Canada

The answer is 1.

Wild axolotls are only found in the waterways of Mexico City.

3. What creatures like to eat baby axolotls?

   1. Water birds
   2. Snakes
   3. Some fish, such as tilapia
   4. Bigger axolotls

The answer is all four! (One point for each correct answer)

Baby axolotls make a tasty and nutritious meal for a lot of river creatures.

4. What kind of habitat do wild axolotls prefer?

   1. Clean, clear water with a strong current
   2. A rock pool near a sandy beach
   3. The murky, shallow Xochimilco river bed
   4. A large aquarium with cool, cycled water, plenty of water plants, and places to hide, properly maintained by a responsible owner.

Axolotl Facts for Kids

The correct answers are 3 and 4.

5. What color is an albino axolotl?

    1. Olive green
    2. Pale pink or white
    3. Copper
    4. It can be any color

The correct answer is 2, pale pink or white.

6. What do most axolotls like to eat?

    1. Sashimi salmon
    2. Blood worms
    3. Sea monkeys
    4. Night crawlers

The correct answer is all of them 1, 2, 3 and 4!

Night crawler worms are an excellent food for adult captive axolotls, but sashimi salmon, bloodworms, and sea monkeys should only be given as occasional treats.

7. How do axolotls socialize in the wild?

    1. They seem to be very competitive and like to race one another.

Answers: Easy Axolotl Quiz

2. They seem to be very sociable and like to live in large communities.
3. They don't.
4. They live in pairs and will remain together for their whole lives.

The correct answer is 3 - Axolotls are solitary creatures that have no need for company.

8. In which range of length is an average healthy adult axolotl?

    1. 5 to 10 cm (2-4 inches)
    2. 15 to 45 cm (6-18 inches)
    3. 60 to 75 cm (24-30 inches)
    4. 80 to 90 cm (32-36 inches)

The answer is 2.

An average, healthy axolotl should measure between 15 and 45 cm from its nose to the tip of its tail.

9. What is the lifespan of a pet (captive) axolotl?

    1. 2 - 5 years
    2. 5 - 10 years
    3. 10 - 15 years
    4. 15 - 20 years

The answer is 3.

Well-cared-for pet axolotls live for around 10 to 15 years in general, although some can live up to 20 years.

10. What status has the International Union for Conservation of Nature given to the axolotl?

1. Critically endangered
2. Vulnerable
3. Near Threatened
4. Least Concern

The answer is 1.

The axolotl is critically endangered in the wild, with only 50 to 1000 individual axolotls remaining in the Xochimilco waterways.

How did you do?

0 - 2 points

Oh dear, you still have a lot to learn about axolotls. Perhaps you need to read this book again!

3 - 5 points

You have a good knowledge of axolotls, but there is still a lot you could learn!

6 - 8 points

Well done! You certainly know a great deal about axolotls!

9 points and over

Answers: Easy Axolotl Quiz

Wow! You really know your stuff when it comes to axolotls!

TRUE OR FALSE?

The axolotls' slime coat may help medical researchers find an alternative to antibiotics?

THE ANSWER IS TRUE. Antimicrobial peptides extracted from the mucous in the axolotl's slime coat could help medical researchers to find an alternative to antibiotics.

Answers: The Hard Axolotl Quiz

Quiz 3 - Axolotls, Test Your Knowledge

The Really, Really Hard One!

1. What is the Latin name (binomial nomenclature) for the axolotl?

    1. Ailuropoda melanoleuca
    2. Ambystoma mexicanum
    3. Ceratotherium simum
    4. Panthera uncia

The answer is 2.

Ambystoma mexicanum is the Latin name for the axolotl.

Answers: The Hard Axolotl Quiz

Ailuropoda melanoleuca is the scientific name for the giant panda, Ceratotherium simum is the white rhino, and Panthera uncia is the snow leopard, all of which are seriously endangered animals.

2. What are iridophores?

    1. Amphibians that gulp their food using their mouths and throats to create a vacuum.
    2. Golden flecks are found on the skin of wild axolotls and some captive breeds.
    3. A type of small, freshwater shrimp that is a good source of protein for axolotls.
    4. Axolotls that continue to metamorphose into salamanders.

The answer is 2.

Iridophores are reflecting pigment cells in several amphibians, some fish, and other creatures such as octopus and squid.

3. What does benthic describe?

    1. An animal with a slime coat.
    2. An animal that gulps its food using suction.
    3. An animal that prefers to live alone.
    4. An animal that lives at the bottom of a body of water.

The correct answer is 4.

The benthic zone is the ecological region at the very lowest level of an ocean, river, lake, or stream.

4. What is the name of the Aztec underworld, with which the god Xolotl is associated?

   1. Mictlin
   2. Hades
   3. Valhalla
   4. Jigoku

The answer is 1, Mictlin.

Hades is the underworld in Greek and Roman mythology, Valhalla is the Viking heaven, and Jigoku is a Japanese mythical underworld.

5. Which of the following organs can an axolotl regrow?

   1. Its brain
   2. Its tail
   3. Its spinal cord
   4. Its eyes

The answer is all four!

Axolotls can regenerate all of their body parts.

6. How many base pairs are in the axolotl genome?

Answers: The Hard Axolotl Quiz

1. 2 billion
2. 13 billion
3. 23 billion
4. 32 billion

The answer is 4.

The axolotl genome has 32 billion base pairs (or 32 gigabytes), about ten times the size of the human genome.

7. Approximately how many species of salamander are there?

1. 360
2. 560
3. 760
4. 960

The answer is 3.

Currently, around 760 species of salamander have been identified.

8. What are the filters in the National Chinampa Refugio project made from?

1. Natural sponge
2. Volcanic rock
3. Recycled aluminum
4. Rock salt

The answer is 2 - Mexican volcanic rock, called tezontle.

How did you do in this harder quiz?

0 - 2 Junior

3 - 4: Learner

5 - 6: Expert

7 - 8: Genius

TRUE OR FALSE?

Charles Darwin suggested axolotls have evolved from prehistoric ichthyostega?

THE ANSWER IS TRUE.

Ichthyostega is one of the earliest known amphibians that resembled a crocodile.

Answers: The Fun Axolotl Quiz

THE FUN QUIZ!

One point for each correct answer!

1. What is strange about Dr. Axolotl, the mad inventor in Disney's animated series, Tailspin?

    1. He can fly
    2. He is a vegetarian
    3. He is actually a lizard
    4. He can't swim

The answer is 3.

Tailspin's Dr Axolotl is not an axolotl, or even a salamander, but a lizard!

. . .

Axolotl Facts for Kids

2. What is the collective noun for a group of axolotls?

   1. An army
   2. A maelstrom
   3. A slumber
   4. A wandering

The answer is 2.

The English collective noun is a 'maelstrom' of axolotls, although some people prefer the alternative, a 'harem' of axolotls.

3. What is the name of the axolotl said to be featured on the Mexican 50 peso banknote?

   1. Melanie
   2. Big Betty
   3. La Gorda
   4. Alexis Pottle

The answer is 3.

Gorda the axolotl, who lives in the Museo del Axolote in Mexico City, is said to have been the model for the axolotl drawing on the Mexican banknote.

4. Which Pokémon is based on an axolotl?

   1. Bulbasaur
   2. Eevee

Answers: The Fun Axolotl Quiz

   3. Lugia
   4. Wooper

The answer is 4.

Wooper is a water/ground-type Pokémon introduced in Generation II

5. According to the popular song, where might you find an axolotl?

   1. On the pink stairs
   2. On the lawn chair
   3. On the high street
   4. At the front door

The answers are 1, 2 & 3.

According to the song, there is no axolotl on the high street!

6. What is the name of the largest recorded axolotl?

   1. Lottie
   2. Axel
   3. Frida
   4. Glob

The answer is 4.

Glob is the name of the largest recorded axolotl.

Glob is a leucistic female axolotl who measures 35 cm (14 inches).

7. What is the rarest axolotl in Minecraft?

    1. Golden axolotls
    2. Blue axolotls
    3. Rainbow axolotls
    4. Translucent axolotls

The answer is 2.

Blue axolotls are very rare, with players having just a 0,83% chance of breeding one.

8. Why shouldn't you take an axolotl on vacation with you?

    1. It is almost impossible to find suitable holiday clothes for them.
    2. They are extremely picky about holiday destinations.
    3. It is extremely difficult to pack an aquarium.
    4. Because it will probably paxalotl!!

The answer is 4.

Although it would be very, very difficult to pack an aquarium!

How many points **did you score?**

0 - 2: Axonotl!

Answers: The Fun Axolotl Quiz

3 - 4: Axolittle!

5 - 6: Axolotl!

7 and over: Axo-lots-and-lotl!

True or False?

The GFP axolotl will glow a luminous pink under ultraviolet or blue light.

The answer is False.

The GFP axolotl will glow a luminous green under ultraviolet or blue light.

And now for a knock-knock joke....

Knock knock!

Who's there?

Axolotl.

Axolotl who?

You sure axolotl questions, don't you? Hahahahah

∽

The final activities!

Activity #1

Try writing your own axolotl quiz, word search, or crossword. Don't forget to use lots of the facts you have learned from this book!

ACTIVITY #2

Why not have a go at creating an axolotl board game? Perhaps it could be a race to save them from extinction, or an adventure game based around an aquarium. Of course, it could just be something colorful, happy, and fun to celebrate your favorite smiley amphibian!

Afterword

Humankind is so lucky to share the planet with such amazing animals as the axolotl.

As well as looking adorable, with its goofy grin and fine, frilly gills, the axolotl is an extraordinary creature that has helped us understand much more about metamorphosis in amphibians and rejuvenation.

Keeping axolotls as pets can be a very rewarding experience, which can help us better understand our environment by creating the right kind of habitat for our "Mexican walking fish." Learning about water quality, testing ammonia, nitrite, and nitrate levels, and working out the perfect diet for your pet can be a fantastic and practical way to understand biology, chemistry, and mathematics. Perhaps it could be the start of a lifetime's appreciation for axolotls and aquarium life, a pathway for higher education, or even a career in that area.

Afterword

However, remember that owning any pet is a significant responsibility. You should always take the greatest care of your pets and make sure you are doing everything you can to keep them happy and healthy.

It is easy to see what makes axolotls so cool, but what really isn't cool is neglecting, being cruel, or eating them. A Japanese restaurant in Yokohama, renowned for serving rare and unusual meats, created a significant controversy in 2025 when it posted pictures of a fried axolotl dish it was serving. Although axolotls (when plentiful) were eaten by some ancient people of Mexico, happily, it seems the world has moved on. There was such an outcry against eating axolotls that the restaurant quickly removed them from their menu.

A lot of people feel just as strongly about helping axolotls in the wild from becoming extinct. Volunteers in Mexico have given their time and expertise in programs and projects that are just beginning to turn the tide. Others have raised funds and spread awareness.

Although we have come dangerously close to losing axolotls in the wild, many conservationists are starting to feel hopeful that it may not be too late for them after all.

With careful conservation, the support of the community in New Mexico, and global efforts to stop global warming, the future no longer looks quite as bleak for axolotls. Especially with axolotl lovers from all over the world doing whatever they can to help.

Thank you so much for reading this book. We hope you have found it helpful and interesting, and that now you feel like you are almost an expert on these fascinating creatures!

Afterword

If you have enjoyed our book, please let us know. We would be delighted - and very grateful - if you would consider leaving us a 5* review on Amazon or wherever you purchased the book from.

www.ingramcontent.com/pod-product-compliance
Lightning Source LLC
Chambersburg PA
CBHW060457080526
44584CB00015B/1457